Intensely practical and insightful,  kind of book all parents should r headstrong children. In an enjoyab personal stories and effective princ_ her own strong-willed children. Her book is full of delightful examples and much needed encouragement that will bring hope to a weary mama's soul.

—Ellen Schuknecht, author of *A Spiritual Heritage: Connecting Kids and Grandkids to God and Family,* mom of 3, grandma of 11

I often joke that the hardest thing I've ever done in my life was not guarding Micheal Jordan or Magic Johnson during my NBA career, but raising four children. Yes, raising children can be that hard! There were many days I felt completely overwhelmed, unprepared, and even at times a failure in my parenting. There were also days I just flat wanted to give up and quit. It was during those difficult times that people like Tami Overhauser, who themselves had been through the battles and came out on the other side, deeply encouraged me to stay in the game. I highly recommend *The Strong-Willed Mama* to those who are starting their parenting journey or are already in the midst of raising their children. You will laugh, cry, shake your head in agreement, and find your own story within Tami's story. In the end, you will walk away with a deep, refreshing hope in your parenting and the understanding that you don't have to walk this journey alone.

—Dave Jamerson, lead pastor, Renovate Church Austin, NBA 1st Round draft choice, author of *Standing Strong in Tough Times,* Dad of 4

Whatever stage of parenting you find yourself in, from toddler to teen & everything between, the life-giving words within the pages of *The Strong-Willed Mama* will encourage you to love hard, fight hard, stay in the ring and show up for the ones who matter. Tami's practical wisdom is rooted in sound Biblical teaching and seasoned by her own experience. Her mother's heart to see healthy families grow is surpassed only by her passion for the greater family of God.

> —Chris Blue, Co-Pastor, Pacific Point Church, CA, co-contributing author of *Mom Mentor What Other Moms Never Told Me,* mom of 5, lala of 1

With the gentleness of knowing there isn't a one-size-fits-all approach but the guidance to light some steps forward on your path, in *The Strong-Willed Mama* Tami takes mama's by the hand and lets us know we're not alone. She is close enough to this season of life to remember how hard it is, but far enough ahead to be able to reassure the ones in the trenches that it does, indeed, get better and we can, in fact, do this.

> —Sarah Sandifer, storyteller, military wife, mom of 3

Parenting is not for the faint of heart, and parenting strong-willed children can be among our toughest battles. In *The Strong-Willed Mama* Tami guides us through the real-life issues our kids face and has made us feel normal in the process. I'm grateful for this important resource and anyone who reads this book will be inspired by her story, her heart, her wisdom, and her love for the Lord.

> —Kim Coya, fitness trainer, nutrition coach, mom of 7

The Strong-Willed Mama is for every mother. Tami courageously shares her most humbling and raw "mom fails" and victories with vulnerability and laugh out loud humor. Her masterful storytelling and wisdom will leave you less critical of yourself and more empowered to face your parenting challenges - no matter what you are facing!

—Sally Scovel, former Olympian, lover of books, mom of 3

When the aftermath of the battle with your strong-willed child comes and you find yourself scrolling through Instagram or Facebook to numb the frustration, pick up this book instead! *The Strong-Willed Mama* will encourage you and prepare you for the next battle at hand. Not many people will share the sometimes ugly truth with you and I found Tami's honesty refreshing! Her words will uplift your spirit and let you know you are not alone. God wants to help change you through the process of raising a world changing (strong-willed) child.

—Rachel Barnwell, friend, realtor, mom of 3

After years of wrangling my own strong-willed children, let me tell you, *The Strong-Willed Mama* will be your lifeline in this season! Tami has a great gift to make you laugh, and her passion for her children is contagious. You'll be blessed, challenged & even relieved to know you aren't alone. We can be STRONG-willed mamas for our kiddos! They need us! Young mamas, get a copy.... Keep it on your nightstand!

—Christina Thomas, fellow NFL wife, interior designer, mom of 4

This fun, honest, and oh so relatable book by a mama sharing her journey of parenting, had me laughing, crying and yelling, "Yes! Yes! Yes!" as I was reading. I began highlighting sections that resonated with me and quickly realized that I was highlighting the whole book! Tami's real-life experiences, combined with her deep faith, send messages of love, patience, forgiveness, and hope for all mamas.

—Jennifer Killian, teacher, encourager, mom of 2

The Strong-Willed Mama takes us on a ride through the ups and downs of motherhood and parenting strong-willed world changers. Encouraging and wise, Tami shares her winning moments as well as her struggles and sprinkles in a good dose of biblical guidance to boot. Get prepared to see "strong willed" in a new light!

—Jodi Fetchel, wellness director, chaos tamer, mom of 3

This book is great! I loved it! So raw and so real! Full of heartfelt stories and relevant biblical truths, *The Strong-Willed Mama* is relatable and encouraging. In an empathetic non-judgmental way Tami shares with us what worked to bring about transformation in her and her family so that we can do the same. We've got this!

—Leslie Harrington, wingman, supporter of dreams, mom of 2

The Strong-Willed Mama is a practical yet hysterical text, all in the same breath! The pages are filled with nuggets of parenting gold! Tami's encouraging words lead you down a path of hope, perseverance and joy, in parenting strong-willed children through some tough seasons, while always directing you back to the Word of God, where true wisdom is found! You will laugh until you cry, then cry until you laugh again! Tami teaches us that in life and in parenting, there are seasons, and if you ask Him, God will work through you to guide your children along His path. She reminded me it is indeed a GOOD THING after all to have a strong-willed child, as long as I am a strong-willed mama!

> —Julia C. Hawthorne, DDS, strong-willed daughter, mom of 2

I love how Tami is able to relate poignant truths with humor and grace in *The Strong-Willed Mama!* This season of life can feel daunting and overwhelming but reading through her tales of woe and triumph gives me hope that I don't have to die on every hill and that God has given me strong-willed babies who will be world changers! Shifting our perspective from "Why are my kids this way?" to "My kids were made this way for a reason!" is life-giving! Strong-willed mamas often want things to go their way, always, and it's just like our God to give us children who remind us how much we need HIM! Tami has been able to glean from her experiences and write a book that is a true blessing for moms trying to navigate raising challenging littles.

> —Anne Barger, lover of Jesus, designer, mom of 3

THE
STRONG-WILLED
MAMA

SURVIVING AND THRIVING RAISING
STRONG-WILLED CHILDREN

*A transformational journey
for the weary mama's soul*

TAMI OVERHAUSER

Cover design by Candor Virtual Marketing, LLC
Interior design & cover edits by Typewriter Creative Co.

All Scripture quotations, unless otherwise indicated, are taken from the Holy Bible, New International Version®, NIV®. Copyright ©1973, 1978, 1984, 2011 by Biblica, Inc.™ Used by permission of Zondervan. All rights reserved worldwide. www.zondervan.comThe "NIV" and "New International Version" are trademarks registered in the United States Patent and Trademark Office by Biblica, Inc.™

Scripture taken from the (NKJV) New King James Version®. Copyright © 1982 by Thomas Nelson. Used by permission. All rights reserved.

Scripture quotations taken from the (NASB®) New American Standard Bible®, Copyright © 1960, 1971, 1977, 1995, 2020 by The Lockman Foundation. Used by permission. All rights reserved. www.lockman.org"

ISBN 978-1-7373952-0-1 (Paperback)
ISBN 978-1-7373952-1-8 (eBook)

CONTENTS

INTRODUCTION

When my oldest son, Adam, was still very young, I began to journal about my parenting journey. I was a busy mom with two little girls, and now this big, beautiful baby boy I had prayed fervently for was in the mix, and I wanted to record every moment. I soon realized that my son had a strong will, unlike anything I'd ever experienced.

Although I considered myself to be a good mom, I was taken aback daily by his dramatic behavior. Everything was a challenge, a fight, and an exhausting battle of wills from sunup to sundown. I wondered if anyone else was struggling the way I was. Was anyone else "white-knuckling" their days, praying and crying through the night? Could there be strength in numbers if I were willing to be transparent with other people? And just how transparent was I willing to be?

Over the years when friends and family would say, "You really should write a book!" I wasn't sure if they thought my parenting tactics were helpful or if my stories were so shocking they deserved to be penned. Either way, I wrote them down—at first for me—and now for you. I turned my raw journaling into a heartfelt blog and, well, my blog into a transparent book, in hopes that someone might benefit from what I'd learned and be encouraged by my stories. Boy oh boy, do I have some stories to tell you!

There are stories about my son's strong will, about the thrill of victory, the agony of defeat, and the transformational work God did in me during what I refer to as the "dark night of the soul." There are stories about how I became a better, stronger version of myself and, in turn, helped my children do the same. There are stories of tantrum-throwing, even poop-throwing, and the first time my child said, "I hate you!" There are stories of my young son exerting his strong will and running away, of me finding the strength to run four miles to bring him back home, and how God transformed my soul in the process.

I will be the first to admit that raising strong-willed children can be frustrating, exhausting, and most definitely humbling. There were days when I thought I had it all figured out, and there were days when I wanted to run away from home! It felt like a never-ending rollercoaster ride at times and a desperately lonely journey at others.

There were moments when I thought:

I must be the only one who has it this rough.

No one else's children act like this.

I am the worst mom!

I could never tell anyone what just happened.

No one would understand: They would just judge me!

It's a toxic, inner dialogue that seeks to further isolate you from the truth and perpetuate a cycle of shame and despair that simply isn't true!

The truth is, you are stronger than you think! It takes a strong-willed mama not to give up when you're weary of doing what the "experts" recommend, just to have frustration set in while the situation seems to get worse—the tantrums, the obstinacy, the yelling on both sides, the endless standoffs and empty threats that leave you bewildered and full of shame. But look at you! Here you are, staying in the fight!

I know your child seems like a fierce tornado that only subsides for the five to six hours they're asleep (if you're one of the lucky ones), returning with a vengeance when the battle of wills continues the next morning. I know you wonder secretly and silently if you will survive another day, let alone eighteen years of this. It's a vicious cycle that you don't want your family to experience but find yourself stuck in nonetheless. Perhaps you even self-medicate while scrolling through feeds of perfect families who seem to be getting it right, leaving you feeling worse off than when you started.

I know! I've been right where you are! If you are like me, you want concrete directions from someone who's gone before you. Some encouragement and support would be nice too. You are not alone. I'm here to help.

In preparing to write this book, I had a long conversation with my dear friend Ellen Schuknecht the dean at Veritas Academy, a private school here in Austin, Texas, where my girls attended early elementary school. She talked, and I gleaned from her years of experience and wisdom. She said the number of strong-willed children born into this generation comes as no surprise to her as she believes it to be God's answer to the cultural depravity and societal erosion in the world around us.

The Bible speaks of the wheat and the tares growing together, and this is exactly that. It takes a strong will to combat what the world is throwing at our kids these days.

It is not our job to break the will or punish it out of our children but to celebrate it and train it and hone it to the service of our Creator.

These children are world changers! Perhaps they are future military leaders, inventors, CEOs, missionaries, movement starters, politicians, and Nobel Peace Prize winners. Dare I say, a strong will may be essential in both them and you. We should want to know what God is doing and get in on it. Well, here is our chance!

But it is not for the faint of heart. Raising my young son felt like facing a huge mountain every morning that I was incapable of climbing. I would run at it full force like a charging bull, only to fall exhausted on the ground every night, feeling as though I'd made zero progress in my attempts to discipline the strong will out of him. The will was ironclad and here to stay! The sooner I realized that, the better off I would be. The key is to *parent* the strong-willed child, not parent the strong will *out* of the child (not an easy task by any means!)

I looked to God for daily strength and patience, reminding myself that God had created my son this way and gave him to me, and I was determined to bring out the best in him. I committed to studying my child to understand him better, bringing love, compassion, patience, and creativity to the table. I learned how to come alongside him, empathize, listen, learn, and find out what makes him tick. God made him intense and passionate, strong and independent on purpose. It was my job to hone those qualities, guide him, and help him navigate his world, not quench his spirit because the task was difficult or inconvenient.

My goal in writing *The Strong-Willed Mama* is to encourage, support, and strengthen you and let you know that you are not alone. (You—can—do—this!) You can even do this and thrive. My son is a teenager now, and we *still* butt heads (there will be a sequel), but during the dark night of the soul, God did a transformational work in us both!

I learned to listen more and yell less. I learned to give grace while setting clear boundaries. Over time we began laughing and playing more than fighting and yelling. He knows he has an advocate and an ear. Over time we've both become less frustrated and angry, kinder and more caring.

In these pages, I am sharing from a place of hindsight and hope. There are short chapters in each section for you to read all at once or one at a time. Read them during naptime, on your coffee break, or in the carpool line. Read them on your porch to your husband or with a friend. I've included some dos and don'ts and some unique ways to bring out the best in your child (as well as yourself) while building a strong healthy family. This book was written for you with your schedule and success in mind. I pray that you feel deeply seen and understood and that this book encourages you to pursue transformation for yourself and your family.

PART 1

LET'S START AT THE VERY BEGINNING

For I am confident of this very thing, that he who began a good work in you will complete it.

Philippians 1:6

1

WE'VE GOT TO PRAY JUST TO MAKE IT TODAY

I have a dear friend whose name is Suzanne (pronounced soo-ZAHN). It's Cajun and unique (as is she). We met on the college campus of Cal State University, Long Beach when I was a junior. She was a cute, newly married thirty-something, who had devoted her life to sharing the gospel with college students. We met weekly for Bible study and became close friends.

She loved working with the college group but longed to be a mom and have children of her own. She worked faithfully and prayed patiently (as she often taught me to do), but it felt like her prayers went unanswered as she attended countless baby showers for her peers. She even watched some of the girls from our college group graduate, get married, and start families of their own. (I promised her that I would wait for her to have a baby before I had one. That's the kind of friend I am.)

She would put on a happy face for the public, but I could sense the devastation in her heart as she and her husband, Gregg, continued to pray, giving it time to happen naturally, trying in-vitro fertilization, and eventually suffering miscarriages. Shortly after Suzanne turned forty-four, they decided to adopt a little girl. Wouldn't you know, while they were finalizing their adoption, they found out they were pregnant! When she told me she said, "I guess I prayed so hard God gave me two babies!"

"Yes ma'am, you sure did!"

Caroline was born in January and Courtney in June of the same year. God answered Suzanne's prayers in ways she never imagined. The years that followed were a bit rough. In her forties dealing with health challenges while managing two babies and a traveling husband, Suzanne found herself yet again on her knees in prayer. This time she asked God for strength just to care for her children.

During that same time, I watched many of my peers find love and get married. I would cry myself to sleep because I wanted desperately to find love and start a family too. Every time a friend would get engaged, I would "tank," call Suzanne, and we would meet for coffee (or chocolate pie if it was really bad!). And she would say, "Tami! Do not cry! That was not your husband! God has your husband just like God had my babies!"

I had a long track record of poor dating decisions, so I figured maybe she was right. I should commit my love life to prayer and see what God had up his proverbial sleeve. What seemed like an eternity of engaged friends, heartache, and chocolate pie, was only a few short years until I met and married the fantastic Chad Overhauser! He was a friend of Suzanne and Gregg, whom I met at a church picnic. He was playing softball with a bunch of friends. There he stood, a football player for UCLA, towering over the others at 6 foot 6 inches and weighing in at well over 300 pounds. It was love at first sight for me.

On our wedding day, I remember waiting in the bridal room with Suzanne by my side as we peeked out the window to watch Chad and his groomsmen take their places in the courtyard of the Sutton Place Hotel in Newport Beach. He stood there so tall and regal in his tuxedo, his shoulders twice the width of some of his buddies. Suzanne and I grabbed hands with tears in our eyes as if we knew what the other was thinking.

My voice cracked as I said, "I think I prayed so hard God gave me two!"

That day truly was a dream come true for me. God answered my prayers beyond what I ever imagined. But the road soon turned bumpy as roads do. God knew exactly what he was doing putting the two of us together, but we seemed to fight over everything and nothing. Chad and I are both considerably strong-willed and stubborn, and our arguments were quite heated. I would call Suzanne for advice wondering how in the world we were going to make it through.

She would remind me of how I stood in faith praying for this man and how God was faithful. The same God who brought Chad into my life, the same God who gave her two babies, is the same God who gives us strength for the journey. She reminded me of what it says in God's Word (it's good to have friends like this!) that he who began a good work will be faithful to complete it, and I can do all things through Christ who strengthens me.[1]

My wedding day and the day my sweet babies were born were miraculous and joy-filled and among the best days of my life, but those days were just the beginning. There would be trials and tribulations, and there would be some dark days. That's just the truth.

My friend, do not lose sight of the Lord, thinking, *Thanks, God. I got it from here.* Rather, call upon his name the way you called upon him in the past, watch and see how faithful he is to walk with you and talk with you and see you through. Ask him to help you once again.

There's a popular worship song entitled "Do It Again" by Elevation Worship.[2] It powerfully speaks of God's faithfulness and proclaims, "I believe I'll see You do it again."

Your promise still stands
Great is Your faithfulness, faithfulness
I'm still in Your hands
This is my confidence
You've never failed me yet
I've seen You move, You move the mountains
And I believe I'll see You do it again
You made a way, where there was no way
And I believe I'll see You do it again.

Many of you are facing mountains in your parenting journey. I know! I've been right where you are. I believe that his promises still stand, and his faithfulness towards you is great. You're still in his hands. He will not fail you. I've seen him move huge mountains in my life and in the lives of others. I am convinced he will do the same for you. He makes a way when there is no way. And he will do it again and again and again!

2

GROWING PAINS

My oldest daughter, Rebekah, was born in Chicago right before my thirtieth birthday. Almost two years later, her baby sister, Samantha, was born right here in Austin. They were sweet babies who loved to sleep and eat and laugh and play. I was on a mommy roll, and there was no stopping me. I planned to have a baby every two years until I had four, maybe five babies. I once told my father-in-law that I wanted ten.

But both my girls were really big babies, and I had rough deliveries. My uterus had prolapsed "like that of a ninety-two-year-old woman," one doctor said. It literally came out with Samantha and was never the same again. (It's fine. I have forgiven her.) The doctor recommended either a hysterectomy or prolapse surgery. I remember frantically calling my friend Chris while driving up the winding road to our home here in Austin (back when it was still legal to be on the phone—not safe, but still legal). I was talking, crying, and driving down this winding road, saying, "Maybe I will just hold my sweet little girls tight and call it a day and get the hysterectomy." She reminded me that I had always dreamt about a big family. I felt that it truly was God's plan for us. (Get some good friends who will remind you of God's plan and remind you of your dreams.)

So, I had the surgery. We called it "Operation Save the Uterus." About a year and a half later, I was pregnant but then soon miscarried. Miscarriages are weird because the minute you find out you are pregnant, you start picking out names and decorating and dreaming, and then, just like that, gone! No one understands because you're not really showing, and the greater extent of the dream lies within your heart.

They say things like, "It's okay. God will give you another baby!" or "You guys are young. You can keep trying."

"Well, it's not okay, *'Karen,'* and I wanted that baby right there! And you should shut your trap! Thanks!"

It seemed like everyone I knew was having a baby, and (to add insult to injury) nine months later the nursery at our church was filled with mostly baby boys. What happened, God? I was going to have babies—and lots of them—remember? There were going to be two, four, six, or eight babies. Someone even said to me, "Oh well, that nursery looks a little crowded with babies anyway."

"I'm sorry, *what?*"

People mean well. They just don't know what to say to you after a loss. After losing a pregnancy, you will never be the same, never take being pregnant or having children for granted again. It is such a delicate process. I sometimes wonder, *How are there even so many people in the world?*

Eventually, I was pregnant again. This time for longer, but not much. I saw the heartbeat a few times (once on my birthday), and the nurses rejoiced with me. I began telling people. Then, two weeks later, there just wasn't a heartbeat. The same nurses grieved with me. I was thankful for their kindness, but I was mad at God. Why did he let me have the surgeries? Why did he give me a desire for more babies? Why did he let me keep trying and see the heartbeat?

It took a while after that last time to get my head back in the game and muster up the faith to ask God for another baby. People were saying, "Call it quits! Throw in the towel, girl. Cut your losses short and count your blessings."

We saw a fertility doctor who told me just what I had thought, that creating life is a delicate process. We put it in God's hands and prayed for the growth of our family and tried to believe our own words when we desperately said, "Your will, Lord, not ours." Before long, I was pregnant again. This time I carried to term, and it was a boy! The showers I was thrown were out of this world as we celebrated like never before. On May 27, 2005, we welcomed Adam Michael Overhauser into the world. Cue the fireworks!

He was perfect and sweet and smiley, and I was over the moon. We felt like our family was complete. We even talked about Chad getting a vasectomy. Then, the very next Christmas with 6-month-old Adam and all my family gathered around, we announced that another sweet baby boy was coming in the summer. (Apparently, you can't just talk about getting a vasectomy.) David Allen Overhauser was born in August 2006. Just like that, we were a family of six.

What is the emotional combination of shock and joy? Awe, I suppose. We were in awe! Even with all the trials we endured to grow our family—boom, just like that—we grew even bigger. God does that sometimes. It's his prerogative, I suppose, to show off his power, his timing, his miracle-working blessings. It's funny to me (divinely planned, probably) how I really hadn't even gotten to know Adam's personality and ironclad will yet, and here I was with yet another baby boy to get to know as well.

These are the situations that keep you on your knees before God in prayer—when the honeymoon wears off, after my friend Suzanne brought two babies home from the hospital, and the time I looked around and realized I now had four children to raise. I still remember the day my husband had to go back to work after David was born. He was all dressed in a suit and white shirt, and I was struggling with the coffee pot.

He looked at me as if to say, "You know I have to go now!"

I looked at him as if to say, "Please, say it isn't so!"

He kissed the top of my head and left for work. There I was, just me and my little bundle of miracles and God. I felt overwhelmed and underqualified for the job. And unbeknownst to me, one of these "miracles" was going to give me a particular run for my money for years to come. I felt like saying, "Wait! Take me with you!" But there was no better place to be.

The Bible says, "Where two or more are gathered together in his name, there [he is] in their midst," and it's true. (Matt. 18:20) I honestly got used to talking to God all day long, asking him to help me and guide me and even restrain me, at times. It often sounded like this: "Well, what now, hmm? What am I supposed to do now? Dear Lord Jesus, help me please."

As my family grew, so did I. I learned how to listen to God and trust him all day long. I learned that I was stronger than I thought, imperfect for sure, but also creative and long-suffering. My own strong will came in quite handy. I felt a new level of maturity come to me.

My teenagers and I have a running joke. I tell them that I can just look at their knees and sense they are about to have a growth spurt. They say, "Mom, my knees hurt!" And I always say, "You're gonna grow soon." God expands and stretches us. Sometimes there is pain. Then all of a sudden, there's growth. When I look back over those early parenting years, I can see the growth.

I see how the little things don't matter so much anymore. I let things go now and don't pick so many battles. I can give room and space for different personalities, foster the uniqueness of each of my kids in a way that uplifts and points them to God rather than exhaust them with unnecessary rules, punishment, and demands. But it happened over time.

There's a phrase I hear a lot in the self-care world. They say, "Grow through what you go through." That rang true for me from those sweet early days in Chicago to the endlessly long days at home here in Austin. (Lots of growth for all of us!)

I think about all the milestones I hit in those early days: nursing, sleeping through the night (my babies and me), bottles, solids, crawling, walking, talking, and potty-training. I always got excited when my children could tie their own shoes and buckle their seatbelts. That felt like growth to me. We celebrate them, don't we? Why? Because it was hard, and we are proud of them! This is the same way God rejoices over us when we grow through what we go through—the fun, memory-making events and the tearful lessons as well.

There will be many opportunities for growth in the years to come. There always is. When you find something that works, when you give grace instead of yelling, when you pray and work hard and see it pay off, rejoice, pat yourself on the back, or maybe get some chocolate pie! Growth in you and your children, albeit painful at times, is cause for great celebration.

PART 2

CONGRATULATIONS! IT'S A STRONG-WILLED CHILD!

Have I not commanded you? Be strong and courageous!
Do not be afraid; do not be discouraged, for the Lord
your God will be with you wherever you go.

Joshua 1:9

3

NAMASTE. THE STRONG WILL IN ME RECOGNIZES THE STRONG WILL IN YOU!

It's hard to pinpoint when I first noticed my son was strong-willed—when I first realized things were different from what I had envisioned, and that a challenge was before me. It's funny how selective the memory can be. I suppose it's God's plan, the same way we don't really recall the pain of childbirth as it's quickly trumped by the joy of a newborn baby. I *do,* however, seem to remember being enamored with my sweet baby boy, who smiled at me and slept through the night. But, even then, there were times when I found him frustrating and difficult.

There was one particularly telling Thanksgiving when Adam was almost two. We love the holidays around here. One set of grandparents would usually come over for Thanksgiving and the other for Christmas, alternating every year. But, for whatever reason, we had no company that year. And to tell you the truth, we were a bit relieved.

Sometimes there are seasons of life where you just need permission not to be "on," permission to stay in your pajamas and focus on your immediate family. If no one has ever given you that permission, allow me to give it to you now! It's okay to honestly say, "This year we need to just hunker down and wait out the storm."

With two little girls, a toddler, and an infant, this was one of those years. We thought maybe Adam had an ear infection because we just could not make him happy. Of course, this was always my thought process whenever my children were fussy and inconsolable. My oldest daughter suffered chronic ear infections until she was about six, and we eventually put tubes in her ears, so I felt like I knew the signs well. I'd much rather believe something was causing my children's bad behavior rather than accept the reality that they were just being bratty.

Adam would screech at this high-pitched octave in his highchair and throw his food off the tray, shaking his head side-to-side. We would say, "No! No!" and put the food back on his tray. And he would throw it off again.

"He's obviously not hungry, so let's let him out of the chair," we would say to each other as if we'd never had a child before, and this was a spectacular, new idea. It *was* new to us.

As anyone with multiple children can attest, every child is different. My first two were rather compliant in their highchair, learning sign language for words like "more" and "all done." Adam wanted nothing to do with sign language, food, or us, so we let him out of the high chair, at which point he would run down the hallway screeching and waving his arms, strongly resembling a pterodactyl.

Nothing was making him happy except playing with his toy cars (which he was doing before we so rudely interrupted him to confine him to the highchair for lunch). What were we thinking? It seemed as if he just wanted something quiet and soothing (you know, because of an ear infection, which he didn't have, by the way).

Looking back, it seems that when life needed us to interrupt him or dictate his schedule, he would buck the system and turn into that angry pterodactyl.

"We are going here now."

"NO!"

"We are doing this now and not that."

"NO!"

"We are eating this and not that."

"NO!"

"We are putting that down and putting this on."

"NO!"

"We are taking a shower, not a bath."

"NO!"

"When did the will show itself strong?" you ask. When it was being crossed! I realized he was strong-willed the minute I chose to cross his will.

"Time to get up."

"NO!"

"Time to go to bed."

"NO!"

And *everything* in between. It was exhausting. Truth be told, this was just the tip of the iceberg, a strong foreshadowing of things to come.

I've learned a lot since that telling Thanksgiving Day— about my son, about myself, what to do, what not to do, and even who to surround myself with to stay encouraged and strong. I know that God made my son who he is. It is my job to parent him and parent him well. I shouldn't fear the strong will. I should embrace and celebrate it!

We watched some old home videos the other day. One of my absolute favorites is where my youngest son, David, about three at the time, has just learned to swim by the steps of the pool, and the older two are taking turns diving. David is being as sweet as can be while I am filming him. Eight-year-old Samantha is there being super maternal, instructive, and patient. Adam is yelling at everyone and trying to get the camera on himself. Then, he dives poorly (because he is only four) and pops up out of the water screaming, "Delete that stupid video because I never want to see it again!"

We laugh so hard every time we watch this because it so beautifully encapsulated their personalities. More than ten years later, they are just about the same. Resign yourself to the fact that you just may have a strong-willed child on your hands who was created that way by God. You have the wonderful responsibility to parent him or her well. And, also, you will laugh about this someday. (I promise!)

4

PARENT THE CHILD YOU HAVE

Can I confess? I have lived in Texas for almost twenty years and have never once taken pictures of any of my children in the bluebonnets. We even had them growing on our property one time. But it never happened, not one picture. I've never even tried. Here's the thing: My family can be feisty. Especially when they were younger, they didn't like to pretend for me, smile for no reason, or pose in uncomfortable clothes while standing in itchy grass. I've come to know our limitations, and I don't sweat it anymore.

But there was a time when I did—sweat it, that is. I longed for the perfect family and the perfect kids. When my kids were little, my husband worked long hours building his company and was rarely home for dinner. I had these lofty dreams of balanced meals, placemats, and dinner-table devotions, none of which happened. I spent night after night serving hot dogs, blueberries, and chocolate milk to little girls who were coloring, accompanied by Polly Pockets and pink ponies, and two strong-willed toddlers in pull-ups who would not sit down for dinner. They stood in the chairs, eating and waving their blue hands at me. I would then wash their hands with a wipe (sometimes using a disinfecting wipe meant for the counters!), put them to bed, and eat my dinner.

Oh, I had my pity parties, for sure. But it was liberating when I realized we were not the dinner-table-devotional type of family. To this day, we don't put much emphasis on the dinner table as a training ground. Though when we do find ourselves together around the table, we cherish it.

On a more serious note, I have had to adjust my parenting style around one very strong-willed child who was easily frustrated and explosive. He did not like surprises or changes in routine. (Neither do I.) I learned not to spring things on him or spontaneously change our schedule. Although things would happen beyond our control every once in a while, as long as I could keep things consistent and give him fair warning of any change, he was much more pleasant to be around.

You do what you've got to do! As a family, we probably haven't entertained at our house or gone to other people's houses as much as I would have liked over the years. Sometimes we had to adjust our plans because it just wasn't going well for him, me, or anyone. I never really made him play with kids he didn't want to, or wear pants with zippers or shoes that had laces because it all led to anxiety, frustration, and anger, resulting in complete meltdowns and arguments.

It took me years to put my finger on it all and wrap my mind around how to raise the child I had (not the one I wished I had or thought I would have). Unmet expectations can lead to such disappointment in life. It's better to let that all go and get to work parenting this child.

I have a dear friend whose daughter is on the autistic spectrum. Her daughter is bright, beautiful, talented, and challenging. I have walked with my friend through diagnosis in elementary school and their difficulties in middle and high school. At each stage, there was a new frustration. She and her husband would remind each other that each stage was going to be different from what they thought. They would have to adjust and do things accordingly. They would raise the child they had, not the one they wished they had.

It has been a victorious battle for us both but a battle nonetheless. It's hard dying to the dream we've had and the life we expected. I have flopped in the chair in my room at almost every season of parenting a difficult child, crying and saying, "I do not deserve this! I did not sow this, and this is not the life I am supposed to be living!" My tears were justified. Your tears are justified. Cry it out if you must. But after we cry it all out, we still have *this* child to not only parent but parent to the point of flourishing.

I liken it to gardening. It is true in a sense; I had not sown this. God sows the seeds, and my job is to tend to the soil, not looking left or right or getting bitter at God for what he has or has not given to me. He obviously thought I was right for the job and that this child and I needed each other. As we take care of the soil (sometimes involving fertilizer, if you will), some gardens will yield sunflowers, and some will yield daisies. Some get crazy crawling ivy that is out of control—yet, oh, so beautiful.

We must not have a case of "the grass is greener on the other side" or pride that says, "Look at me and my beautiful roses." We aren't in control of the seeds that were sown, but we are responsible for providing good soil and tending to what grows. We are charged with nourishing and nurturing them and building a foundation where they can thrive.

I wish I had a formula for instant success. Here's the kicker: each person's garden is unique and requires specific care. (Aargh! I know, right? Not the answer you were looking for!) Here are a few sure-fire ways to get started, though:

- Do not neglect the garden because that won't work, no matter who you are!

- Lay down your pride and your dreams of *the child you wish you had.*

- Study your child.

- Purpose to find out what makes him or her tick and thrive and flourish.

- Be his or her hero.

- Seek help (professional, if necessary, as well as from supportive family and friends who've gone before you).

- Pray without ceasing.

My friend and I still talk often about what things might look like today if we kept trying to parent the children we wished we had. It brings us to tears talking about the days we wanted to give up altogether and the negative impact it would have made in our children's lives and conversely, the fruit we see now because we chose to push up our sleeves, get our fingernails dirty, and tend to our beautiful gardens.

5

BEING STRONG-WILLED DOES A BODY GOOD. PASS IT ON!

Over the years when I've heard people talk about a strong-willed child, it often seemed to be in a negative light as if it's a bad thing—a disorder or an imperfection of sorts. It can even be conveniently used as an excuse for poor behavior. (I am guilty as charged on that one, for sure!)

"Oh (enter nervous laughter), I'm sorry. He is just very strong-willed."

While I was pregnant with the first of my four children, I read *The Strong-Willed Child* by Focus on the Family founder, Dr. James Dobson, in preparation for what might come. My husband and I were quite strong-willed children. Honestly, we were strong-willed adults, so I figured our poor kids had as much chance of inheriting a strong will as they had of getting blonde hair and blue eyes. *(Eh-hem!)* And I had better get ready!

My friend Suzanne likes to joke, "What'd ya expect when you mixed fire and gasoline!" That's a good point, and I do think being strong-willed has gotten a bad rap. Perhaps being strong-willed can be a good thing.

I began to see the term in a different light one day while dropping my boys off at preschool. I was exhausted from a battle of wills with two preschoolers, and the school day hadn't even started yet! Imagine being exhausted before

9 a.m. I mean, I got whacked in the face with a backpack strap just trying to get out of the car in the parking lot. It left a huge welt. (And let me tell you, I believed it to be no accident!)

Once I made it safely inside the preschool doors, I began to cry and vent to the lovely and sympathetic owner of the preschool. She dried my tears and said, "Well, what do you think you are raising here, a bunch of wimps?" She began to tell me about her own strong-willed son (now grown) and all the positive qualities he had that served him well over the years, and what a fabulous adult he had become. Then she said, as she always did, "Now run along. You only have four hours." Gosh, I loved her! Her hindsight and perspective were just what I needed. She truly made the preschool years with strong-willed boys much more bearable for me.

I know raising a strong-willed child can be difficult, exhausting, and even humbling, but fear not! Being strong-willed can also be a good thing. Think about it:

- Strong leadership resides inside the strong-willed child. The world needs good, strong leaders, and it needs you to raise them!

- The strong-willed child will not take "no" for an answer (which might frustrate you now but will come in handy in the future).

- The strong-willed child does not conform to the "status quo," and peer pressure is hardly ever a problem. My children rarely follow the pack and are not shy in sharing their opinion and paving their own road.

- The strong-willed child will persist at their problems until solved, such as learning to ride a bike, shoot baskets, serve a volleyball, and even build a Lego tower. Great pride comes when their tenacity and follow-through pay off.

- The strong-willed child will stand up for themselves and others. It takes great courage to not care what others think of you as you engage in an act of kindness or bravery.

- The strong-willed child tends to be independent and self-sufficient early on. I am picturing my 2-year-old saying, "I do it myself, Mama!" or my son always asking the grocery store clerk at H-E-B if he can have a Buddy Buck or a balloon at just three years old.

- The strong-willed child when nurtured, loved, and encouraged, is full of life, confidence, and adventure.

- God can use a strong will turned toward him to do mighty things.

- Strong-willed children keep you on your toes. And they keep you on your knees (in prayer).

- Embracing the journey to parent a strong-willed child can make you a better parent and a better person.

- Your own strong will comes in handy when parenting your children.

This child is strong and full of life and potential. See it as a good thing. Raising him or her is a privilege and a high call. We have been given the opportunity to shape and mold the future leaders of the world. Being strong-willed is not bad. Your child is not bad. You are not a bad mom! Embrace the task at hand!

6

BECOMING BADASS

One summer, shortly after my twenty-first birthday, I accompanied my ever-adventurous dad on a houseboating trip to Lake Powell with some of his work friends and their families. Because I shared my dad's love for water-skiing, and my mom did not, she was more than happy to let me take her place as his "plus one." They were a rowdy, beer-drinking, river rat bunch, with whom I found myself very comfortable. At first, they thought I was there to babysit their children, but I quickly set them straight and spent most of my time drinking beer out of the bottle and sunning myself on the top deck of the houseboat with a large, hairy, tan dude in a Speedo, named Pinky.

One day my dad popped his head up and announced he arranged an adventure for us all.

"Get up! Today we're gonna learn how to parasail!" he said.

I had only seen people parasailing from afar on a big stretch of beach in Mexico and also in Hawaii. Each time I watched while they stepped into a harness attached to a parachute and ran while an instructor ran alongside them. Then the boat magically and effortlessly lifted them into the air. And away they flew, with their friends and family cheering them on from the boat below. What fun! Count me in!

We loaded up our ski boat and drove until we found a very narrow cove with cliffs on either side—more of a valley—not at all like the beaches I had seen in Mexico or Hawaii. So I was apprehensive when I realized I was supposed to go first. I reluctantly hopped out of the boat and was handed my harness and parachute, only to turn around and see my dad and four middle-aged men trying to read an instruction manual like it was written in Chinese. This could not be a good sign. Where were the expert instructors to run alongside me? Were we literally going to learn how to parasail on the fly?

Standing alone in what I had now nicknamed "The Valley of the Shadow of Death," Apparently, I was going to learn how to parasail on the fly! I looked down at the apparatus I had strapped myself into and then back at the boat full of novices and thought a few things:

I can't believe they talked me into this!

They have no idea what they are doing!

I have no idea what I am doing!

There is no turning back now!

Tell Mom I love her!

They were all yelling different instructions at me, but above it all, I heard my dad yell, "Just Run!"

I ran a few short feet before belly-flopping into the murky water when Pinky hit the gas, accelerating the boat and dragging me along face first! I was sure this was very wrong and nothing like what I had seen on vacation. I hadn't seen the adventurous folks in Mexico getting waterboarded before being violently catapulted thirty feet into the air.

Once in the air, my torture continued. I opened my eyes to see a cliff three feet from my face! I heard my dad's voice again from the boat, this time yelling, "Push off! Push off!"

Push off? Did it say that in the instruction manual?

I stuck my little leg out and pushed off the rocky cliff. It was either that or smack right into it like Wile E Coyote. I pushed, and the boat pulled, and we emerged safely from the cove. And, lo and behold, I was parasailing! That's one way to do it, I guess.

I had indeed cheated death that day. But from high in the sky, I could see for miles, and the feeling of flying was exhilarating. I was actually quite proud of myself for surviving. I could see the guys in the boat cheering and high-fiving down below. Although they may have been prouder of themselves than they were of me, there was great celebration going on in the boat. (I'm no expert. But I think they needed to work a little on the landing because I'm reasonably sure you aren't supposed to drag your para-sailer for another half mile, and a lake-water enema isn't part of the re-entry process.)

Later that day Pinky and I resumed our place as king and queen of the houseboat, and he offered up a toast.

"To you!"

"To Me!" I laughed, recalling the day's events.

"You did that, girl!"

"Yes, I did!"

"You're kind of badass!"

"Yes, I am!"

I never saw Pinky and the gang again after that trip, nor have I parasailed again. But my dad and I will always have that wonderful memory. We like to tell the story every chance we get to anyone who will listen because it was grand and dramatic and made me feel, strong, fearless and, yes, badass!

Parenting can feel like that too, can't it? It can be grand and dramatic and not at all what you expected! You look at the little baby you just brought into the world and think, *I don't have a clue what I am doing! How did I get talked into this? Where is the instruction manual? Where are the experts to run alongside me?*

Oh, you've heard about it and even observed other moms at the park or the mall. You thought you knew what it would be like, but you truly had no earthly idea what was about to come your way. How could you? You never *quite* know until you personally experience it. You're going to have to learn some stuff on the fly. But in doing so, the miraculous happens. You figure it out! And it's there that you become strong and find your resilient, badass self.

How do we get stronger?

By doing hard things.

How does one learn to parasail?

By parasailing.

Apparently, on the fly!

Without an expert!

When I was pregnant for the first time with my daughter, Rebekah, I longed for an expert to run beside me. We had just moved from California to Chicago, where it was freezing. I was homesick, lonely, and unquestionably pregnant! I made a sweet friend, Michelle, whose husband played football with Chad. Michelle happened to be a labor and delivery nurse. And she, too, was expecting her first baby. Hello, expert!

We would shop together, get lunch, and compare our pregnancy stories. She seemed so confident and knowledgeable, more so than I felt anyway. She would tell me stories from the labor, delivery, and recovery room to help me prepare for the experience. I did all but take notes. When she brought her own sweet 7-pound baby boy into the world, her calm rather textbook experience encouraged me and made me feel ready to go.

One afternoon after lunch at Ruby Tuesdays, I said to her, "Okay, I think I can do this!"

She laughed and said, "I'm glad to hear that! You do realize there's no turning back now, right?"

"Right..."

My sweet Rebekah was due in May and arrived two weeks later on June 12, weighing in at 9 pounds 3 ounces. She actually did not come on her own. We had to induce labor to help her along. It took three days and the use of forceps to get her out! (Forceps are like salad tongs but much bigger. I don't think they use them anymore.) I was admitted to the hospital on a Thursday to start induction, and Rebekah was born on a Saturday.

I was not allowed to eat once I arrived at the hospital in case I would need emergency surgery. I almost wasted away while watching meal after meal constantly being delivered to this large NFL player patiently sitting next to me. Somewhere around day two, I found myself bursting into tears while staring at a piece of banana bread from the cafeteria left carelessly on a tray. I muttered, "Why won't they let me eat?"

To make matters worse, the epidural I received hit a nerve it shouldn't have. Now not only were my legs numb, but I had a splitting "spinal headache" from the experience. It's like a migraine but worse because I was in labor and my legs were numb. I should have known something was wrong when the anesthesiologist blew into my room like the circus coming to town, announced himself as Dr. Doberman, spun me around, gave me an epidural, and pinched a nerve in my spine in the process.

Despite paralysis and starvation, on Saturday morning, June 12, 1999, I pushed, and the doctor pulled. And big, beautiful Bekah reluctantly made her way into the world! There was a moment of celebrating and rejoicing in the room, and then I was quickly whisked away for a small procedure to stop the spinal headache. Once back in my room while the feeling returned to my lower body and my well-fed husband snuggled with his newborn baby girl, you'd better believe I ate that 3-day-old banana bread like it was my job.

All the stories in the world could not have prepared me for that weekend. I had to experience it myself. And do you know what? I tell that story over and over again to anyone who will listen because it is grand and dramatic and makes me feel strong, resilient and, yes, badass. All moms should feel badass! Giving birth is no joke! It's why we swap labor stories *all* the time. That is some dramatic stuff, and I love how proud we are of each other.

It's funny how after a while giving birth doesn't seem like the hard part of this gig. The focus eventually turns from that one dramatic moment in the delivery room to the valley you find yourself in with your little strong-willed child. You're knee-deep in it now, and some days it may even feel like you are getting dragged face-first through the murky water. Dig deep, mama, and remember what you've already been through—what you know you are capable of. You are strong and resilient. Stick your little leg out and push off that proverbial cliff. You can do this!

Another defining moment for me came one day when my strong-willed son was just six years old. He liked to run from me any chance he got. He would not stay in the sandbox or on the jungle gym at the park, like everyone else. Instead, he would run from me as far and as fast as he could until he was out of sight. There was no standing and shooting the breeze with the other moms for me, which was particularly frustrating with multiple kiddos in tow. He would run from me in the mall or parking lots. He would even run from us at home when he didn't want to listen.

This particular day he jumped on his bike and declared he was running away from home—no luggage to speak of but running away nonetheless. It was in the heat of summer, and all he had on were jean shorts, no shoes or shirt or helmet! I wonder if you've ever felt the way I felt that day.

With his little brother by my side and some onlooking neighbors, I chased him down the street a few blocks until he was out of sight. My frustration turned into anger; then my anger turned into worry.

Where will he go?

Is there a car coming?

Will he dare leave the neighborhood?

Why is this my life?

Standing there helplessly, I was still in a place of unbelief. It is so hard coming to terms with the lengths some children will go to assert their will. I sat in the front yard crying and praying. I waited around a bit in the park directly across the street from our house, letting his brother play on the swing. Adam eventually came back zooming full speed down the street. He made the loop around the park a handful of times, laughing and sticking his tongue out at me.

As I sat there feeling held hostage by his antics, I knew I had to do something. *I am a strong, capable woman,* I thought to myself. *I need to take control of this situation!* I did not narrowly escape death by parasailing and three days of starvation in an Illinois hospital to be taken down by an unruly 6-year-old on a BMX bike. *Not today, Satan!*

I stood still in the park as he got closer and closer, buzzing the tower and sideswiping me with his bike. I studied his rhythms like trying to find the right time to step into a revolving door. Here he comes again and again and again! Not yet, not yet—now! I jumped onto the sidewalk and ran alongside him for a hot minute before grabbing the back of his shorts, pulling him from his bike, gathering his brother from the swing, and taking them both back into the house in one fell swoop.

Oh, I'm sure someone was watching me. Normally, I would be mortified, but that day I did not have time to care what people saw or thought. "Go back in your houses everyone. The show's over folks!" I was doing the best I could and then some. In fact, I felt kind of badass. As if the theme song from *Cops*[1] should be playing in the background, "Bad boys, bad boys! Whatcha gonna do when they come for you?"

Look, the last thing I wanted to do that day was track down my son like some kind of bounty hunter, but there was no instruction manual telling me what to do when my son runs away. I was learning on the fly once again, so I dug deep and rose to the occasion. I could imagine my dad yelling, "Just run!" and my friend Michelle saying, "There's no turning back now!" I was indeed becoming the strong-willed mama that I needed to be to raise this very strong-willed child.

I actually had it in me all along. On that day, a glimpse into who I truly was and what I was capable of shone through and gave me a glimmer of hope. It was all going to be okay. I was proud of myself. I stayed in the fight that day, and my new victory felt good and gritty. It felt like boat-top beer bottles and well-earned banana bread on my baby's birthday. I felt pretty badass that night as I washed my hands of the day's dirty work with a smile on my face, humming the theme song to *Cops*.

PART 3

GROW THROUGH WHAT
YOU GO THROUGH

Consider it all joy, my brothers and sisters, when you encounter various trials, knowing that the testing of your faith produces endurance. And let endurance have its perfect result so that you may be perfect and complete lacking in nothing.

James 1:2-4 (NASB)

7

TAKING IT ALL IN STRIDE

All of my babies were sweet, sleepy, fat, and happy. Hate me if you will; it's just how they were. Adam was no different. In fact, he wasn't much of a challenge until he was crawling. Even then it was just him exploring a lot of staircases and me having to buy a lot of baby gates. But when he was just fourteen months old running around with his strong will emerging while I cared for my newborn, Adam became quite the task. Thank God for grandparents!

What a blessing it was to have my parents pinch-hit for me in that season. My parents came into town to take care of the kids, and right after that my mother-in-law came to visit too. I developed a horrible staph infection in my C-section incision and had to receive treatment from a nurse every day. The doctor said I had the option of returning to the hospital with my baby until the infection cleared up or visiting the doctor every day. A third option was eventually given where a nurse would come to my home to clean it out every day until it healed.

Lovely! Door Number 3, please!

No sooner did I choose option 3 than I began to regret it. As nice as it was to have house calls, my children would knock on the door every single morning while a strange nurse cleaned out the pus from my incision. She eventually taught my husband how to do it. And he took it from there, which felt like having my diaper changed by a cute, hunky football player every morning and night while my baby cried and while my toddler stuck his fingers under the door screaming, "Want Mama!" (Good times!)

Sometimes your children have done nothing wrong. But life seems hard, so they seem hard, and you take it out on them. More often than not, I look back on situations like this and think, "Yeah, that was definitely all me and not them at all!" I was thankful my mother-in-law was there to help with the kids while my husband changed my diapers.

After a while, I was ready to get out of the house. I always think I am ready for an outing when really, I am not. I have a friend or two who get up and go right after they have a baby. I always think I can do that too. But when I do, I turn into a hot, sweaty, hormonal mess and look for the closest door out of wherever I am, and then feel horrible about myself. *Why am I not like them? Those new moms who can just get up and go, whose bodies bounce right back?* But because I had been cooped up so long with the C-section situation, I set out to prove I could be just like them.

I was surely deserving of an outing. It was summer, and the kids had been sitting with me in my bed or on the couch for what seemed like months. Plus, whenever I have relatives visit, I always feel the need to "get up and go" because if I don't, then everyone sits on the couch staring at me. I'm already a three-ring circus, and now I have invited people to buy a front-row ticket to watch "the crazy lady spin her plates." I'd rather go on outings!

Out we went to the mall to buy Adam his first pair of shoes. I was pregnant with David for most of the first year of Adam's life. That summer was super hot and also the rainiest summer on record, so we were inside a lot. It had dawned on me that I had never bought Adam any walking shoes. He had some sandals he wore to church but nothing else. Every time I said that to people, they would look at me like they were thinking, *How is this child fifteen months old and has never had shoes?*

For my big outing, I wore a pair of jeans, fully ignoring, of course, the baby weight still on my hips, the big gauze bandage across my tender C-Section situation, and the fact that it was August in Texas and 110 degrees! But we do these things, don't we? Why do we do these things?

My mother-in-law and I arrived at Stride Rite with my boys riding tandem for the first time in my new double stroller. David was crying, and I let my barefoot toddler loose in the store so he could try on the shoes. He looked so big and sturdy and handsome in the pair we finally picked. He kept trying to run out of the tiny store, and my mother-in-law kept heading him off at the pass. I remember her saying to me, "Okay, Dear, we had better pay and wrap it up here!" I could feel the chaos brewing and the sweat starting to drip down my brow, not to mention the bandage under my tight jeans was feeling the need for a change. My body felt cold and clammy. *Too soon! Too soon!* I thought. *Why do I do this to myself?*

No sooner had she spoken than Adam took off running at top speed. He did not care that I had yet to pay for his shoes or that "Mommy can't run right now!" He ran so fast, straight to a bench that looked over the railing to the lower level as my mother-in-law chased after him. Bless her heart! I watched it all in slow motion as he climbed up on the bench to see what was down there, and my mother-in-law snatched him up by the back of his shirt.

I stood in the store feeling helpless with my half-empty double stroller, in my sweaty gauzy jeans, listening to my crying baby.

What have I gotten myself into?

Why is he like this!

My girls never did this!

Is this just boys versus girls?

The reality is I was beginning to see just how strong-willed he was, and it wasn't going to change anytime soon. It strikes a selfish chord in us when situations don't work out the way we want them to, doesn't it? There will be plenty of opportunities for outings and chores and visiting and shopping over time. I promise you. Just because *you* want to do something right now doesn't always mean it's the best choice for the good of the whole.

Sometimes it helped me to make lists, especially as a stay-at-home mom. Often it was just to organize my day, so it didn't drag on endlessly. But it was also to assess what needed to be done and weigh it against my energy level and the temperament of the children at home with me. Then I had to be honest and ask myself some revealing questions: What do I *have* to do? What do I *want* to do? What feels like striving? Then I'd start taking things off the list.

It's a shocking realization upon having children that your life is not your own. I remember an incident right after having my first child. It was my husband's birthday, and I wanted to make him a cake. I just remember looking at sweet Rebekah Lynne sleeping, the clock, my car keys, and back at the baby over and over again until I started to sob. We laughed about it when Chad got home. I was still sitting there crying, with no cake to speak of. Oh, what I would have given for a little Instacart, DoorDash, or Amazon Prime back in the day!

Your life is not your own, and no one knows that better than the mom of a strong-willed toddler. After our youngest was born, my husband and I tried to take all four kiddos out to dinner. Grandma had already left our house and gone back to hers. We were on our own, and we thought we were ready! I remember it so well. We went to Salt Grass here in Austin. The girls were coloring, the baby was crying, and Adam would not stay in his highchair. We were all together, but the time was not quality time. Chad was frustrated. I was hormone sweating. We looked at each other and said, "Too soon? Too soon!" and left before our drinks even came. Why torture the whole family? Trust me, no one was happy! Save your sanity and money for a date night.

Just the other day, we were out to brunch with our now grown daughters and teenage sons (see how effortless that sounded?) and there was a table behind us with a young family trying to enjoy their time together. The poor mom had a newborn and a very lively little girl who would not stay in her seat and kept coming to say "hi" to us. Both parents looked so overwhelmed and miserable. I smiled a smile of grace and comradery and made eye contact with the young mom.

"Oh my God, I don't even know what to do!" she said.

"You are doing great," I said, "but sometimes serving chicken nuggets in front of the TV sounds easier, doesn't it?"

My husband and I laughed about it later. We were both glad to be over the hump on this particular issue. Looking back, we should have had more takeout on the front or back porch, or maybe hired more babysitters. I do realize that some folks like to go out or meet up with family and friends. You just have to find what works for you and your family. Find your little grace lane and run in it. Remember that your life is not your own, but this is just a season. There will be plenty of opportunities for family dinners out. I promise you that even the strong-willed ones will eventually sit around the table with you at a restaurant.

8

BECOMING HUMBLE

Back in college, I used to babysit for my hairdresser in exchange for haircuts. I'm still not sure who was getting the better deal. I remember one time when I took her two young kids to the park and then out to McDonald's. I was standing in line with the little boy by my side, holding his little sister on my hip, and across from me in line was this super cute guy. We smiled at each other a few times. Just as I was feeling good about myself like I was some kind of hot nanny effortlessly multitasking, the little girl leaned over and said at the top of her lungs, "Ew! Miss Tami, your breath smells disgusting!"

I should have seen it as a foreshadowing of things to come. Parenting can be humbling, even darn right embarrassing at times! Just when you think you've got it all together, someone poops or throws up or kicks you in the shins at the worst possible moment. I remember that day at McDonald's often and laugh. Hey, at least their mom was coming at 5:00 p.m. to pick them up.

Early on in my parenting journey, my outings were constantly sabotaged by my strong-willed toddler. It rocked my world for a long time. When my girls were little, I could take them on errands or to coffee with a friend, and they would entertain themselves with a doll or some coloring books. I could even take them to Target if I got them a muffin or a smoothie. Not so with my boys! My boys would devour muffins like Tasmanian devils, leaving a trail of crumbs behind and poking holes in the bottom of the cup spilling smoothie everywhere, all before we hit the dollar aisle.

I always seemed to be at Target when we encountered onlookers and their comments: "Hang in there, Mom!" or a singsongy, "Looks like someone is ready for a nap!" and the ever-popular, "Wow, you sure have your hands full!" These comments always struck me as funny because I would be thinking, *I'm doing pretty good considering the screaming monster I have held hostage in my little red cart here, and you have no idea how much worse this could get.* But as a struggling young mom, it also made me feel kind of bad about myself. So much shame would set in right there. I feel like Target should be a judgment-free zone, maybe have staffers to encourage you at every turn: "You go, girl! You're doing great! No judgment here!"

I told you before that my son was a runner. He ran like Forrest Gump—in parks, grocery stores, parking lots, malls, and on beaches! I should have swallowed my pride years ago and purchased that teddy bear backpack leash. You know the one I am talking about! But at the time, I felt it looked like bad parenting. Somehow it represented my surrender—that I could not make him stay next to me or hold my hand. Gosh, how I must have jerked the heck out of his little arm while staring at him with my tight-lipped, disapproving face trying to get him to "Obey Mommy!" and "Stay!" (Ugh! Hindsight is so lovely, isn't it?)

It seemed to me that the backpack leash moms had given up. There she was in the dairy aisle just picking out her eggs, paying *no attention* to her kid—because...he...was...on...a...leash! (Oh, the bliss of defeat.) Not me! I'm a good mom over here training my child at all times (or squeezing his arm, scowling at him, chasing, threatening to spank, and then *maybe* following through when I get home). Who is the bad mom now? But I just couldn't bring myself to do it— the backpack leash that is. I was too frustrated and proud! Shouldn't my son be able to stay by my side? Maybe, but if I needed some help, that's okay.

Don't be afraid to do what it takes to help your child succeed, no matter what people might say or think about you. The backpack leash is just one example. They don't know what you're struggling with and most likely have their own struggles. Who knows, seeing you fight for your child might be liberating to them. People will say what they will. You don't have any control over that. What you do have control over is your response to your strong-willed child and how you help him or her succeed.

Maybe it's Murphy's law or maybe just my bad luck, but it seemed like anytime someone came to my door, my boys turned into circus performers. Does this happen to you? To no avail, I would beg the boys to behave and even role-play how we act when someone comes to the door. Then I would brace myself, open the door, and try to ignore them. "Nothing to see here!" I remember the gut-wrenching stress level of trying to manage my boys, pretend everything was fine, and talk to my visitor. I wonder if they could tell how much of an internal wreck I was.

I remember one mom glancing over my shoulder with a look of concern at the half-naked acrobats yelling obscenities and performing for an audience behind me. She proceeded to point-blank ask me if my son had ADHD. And before I could answer, she told me a story about the Olympic swimmer Michael Phelps and how "he had ADHD, you know, and his mom just threw him in the water one day, and now look! You should get him into swimming!" I thought to myself, *Maybe, but why? So I could have an Olympic swimmer with ADHD? Or maybe they just need me to not answer the door at dinner time and pay more attention to them. Thank you, and goodnight.*

But that's not what I did. I silently suffered through the conversation, closed the door, and cried in a heap on the floor, feeling like a failure. Even blaming the boys! Face it. Your kids will embarrass you. It's a given with a strong-willed child. It doesn't mean you are a bad mom. You are not a failure. I used to think my little girls were so compliant and perfect because I was such a *good* mom. This mom stuff was so easy! If that line of reasoning were true, when my son's behavior was so bad, it would have been because I was a *bad* mom doing a horrible job. Again, simply not true! I was out there doing the very best I could, in a challenging, humbling, season, to train my children and love my family well. No mom is perfect, and no child is perfect. I was not a failure. You are not a failure. Let your pride go!

Through the years I have gained a lot of compassion for moms going through what I went through. Now, when I see you out and about, I try to smile and offer a look of solidarity and comfort. No one needs to field snarky comments on their family outing to Costco. One way to cope is to develop a sense of humor and use a few key phrases to respond to onlookers:

Thanks, we're good.

Yes, parenting is hard isn't it? Pray for us!

Oh, ya know, what's a girl to do?

Hey, you should see us on a bad day!

My boys went through a phase where they called everyone and anyone a "poopy-doody head," and then they would laugh hysterically. I was horrified at the time until one day someone was really offended, and I decided to lighten the mood by saying, "Be glad that's all he called you!"

These days my favorite phrase is, "Gosh, parenting is hard, isn't it?" It seems to be a moment of truth that brings compassion and stops negative comments.

"You carry on now and have a nice day, sir!"

This is just a season. Albeit a humbling one, children go through seasons and phases. It can be liberating and empowering when you stop worrying about the onlookers and the naysayers, keeping in mind, you don't need to go home with *them,* but you do need to go home with *your child.* Continue to find what works for your family, give each other the gace and the space to be imperfect while you grow, and you will sleep soundly at night knowing you honored yourself, your child, and God.

9

BECOMING FLEXIBLE

When my daughter Samantha was younger, she was a super picky eater. I remember a season where all she would eat were bananas and hot dogs. I quickly grew weary of her finicky ways because I'm not out here trying to make six different dinners. I decided to draw the line. "You will eat what you are served, missy!" She did not like this idea one bit and would sit at the table for what seemed like hours crying and staring at a piece of broccoli. And she *really* hated my chicken.

One time in particular when my mom was visiting, we were serving chicken for dinner. We reminded Samantha that she was to eat everything on her plate, even the chicken! She began to dramatically explain to her grandma how she couldn't possibly bring herself to eat it, and so began what is now referred to as "the gray wad standoff."

Samantha proceeded to gently chew the chicken while simultaneously pretending to gag. It was quite the show! (She has since gone on to win many awards for her theatrical performances. Let it be known: It started here folks.) It eventually became just a gray wad that oozed out of the corners of her mouth, but I remained unflappable. "Eat your chicken, Samantha, and then you can be excused," I said. She looked at me with puppy dog eyes and back again at her grandmother.

Long after everyone else had cleared their plates and left the table, my sweet mom, who had been silent up until now, yelled out, "Dear God, let the child spit it out!" It was a ridiculous standoff to my mom and a bit ridiculous to me now ten years later. Samantha still claims it was very dry chicken.

I loosened up over the years because, the truth is, all four of my kids have their food likes and dislikes. Don't we all? I've certainly learned what not to serve, and they have learned how to be polite at the dinner table and at least try new things. I'm pleased to tell you that they are all healthy, strong, thriving young adults. Mission accomplished! They even eat fruits and vegetables. (Well, we are still working on the teens.)

The issue is not the food, is it? The issue is the desire to be in control and have our children obey. And when they don't, we get frustrated and angry. This is when seeing the big picture and learning to pick my battles came into play. I learned that it's okay not to die on every single hill. I know it's tempting, but it's exhausting. Save it for really big issues. Dry chicken is not one of them.

Double Trouble. When my boys were old enough to sleep through the night, I thought it would be a fun idea for them to share a room. (Not to mention, six of us lived in a four-bedroom house. Someone had to share!) The girls had done it before with no problems other than lots of giggles and a few reminders of house rules. What could go wrong?

I went all out and made a western-themed bunk room for my little cowboys. It was dreamy in so many ways. It was great for bathing, changing, and putting away laundry. But when it came down to the actual sleeping, it was an absolute nightmare! Once we read *all* the books and said *all* the prayers; once they were "snug as a bug in a rug" one little cowboy would *saunter* downstairs like clockwork, complaining that someone threw a sock, or was mean or wouldn't stop talking or stop looking. There were even fistfights! The number of times I climbed the stairs each night could've counted as a hearty workout and made a grown man weep. Again, *I* was determined to make it work, so I would drag little cowboys back to bed, console, reprimand, even threaten them multiple times a night every night. When it got really bad, I made up the day bed in my office for whoever just "couldn't take it anymore" or whoever was downstairs when I "lost it." Then my husband and I got this crazy idea to convert my office into a bedroom for one of the boys. We have not had a problem since! Well, not *that* problem.

I wish my cute bunk room idea had worked. It had been a dream of mine since I dreamt of having two boys. I kind of wanted to die on the hill fighting for it, but I was about to die on the stairs, honestly! So I had to compromise. Sometimes it's okay to compromise and take the easy way out.

Early on, my husband would argue that I'd "gone soft," and it wasn't fair that Adam got the big room all to himself. Truthfully, David didn't mind the office. He said he liked the fact that it had a flat-screen TV and was closer to the refrigerator. Think win-win! They stop fighting, and we get to sleep.

It's not really about the sleeping arrangements, is it? It's about letting go of expectations. It's about picking your battles and finding your sweet spot of compromise and peace. We still read stories and prayed together. Then off they went to their separate rooms. They even missed each other and asked for sleepovers! I didn't miss my office either. On most days I would just sit at the kitchen table to work. It's closer to the refrigerator!

Naps. I feel the same way about nap time—blessed nap time! Why is it such a thing? I would go to great lengths to get a toddler to nap. Interestingly enough, I had two children who loved to nap and two children (much like adults, I suppose) who just would not nap unless they were extremely exhausted or sick. I am not much of a napper and never have been, but I do love some peace and quiet. I would feel very accomplished if I could get a toddler to nap for an hour, even if it took us both a hot, sweaty, 45-minute tantrum to get there.

I wonder now if it was even worth it? Sometimes my son would appear ten minutes later asking if nap time was over. You know you've been there. Maybe you are there right now. Did I feel accomplished because I got my way or because they needed the rest? Did *they*—or did *I?* I came to realize that it was *me* wanting them to act the way *I* thought they should act and for the day to go the way *I* thought it should go, and I was angry and frustrated if it did not. The day was a loss. My child was disobedient, and I was a failure.

Much like with dinner table struggles, stop here and ask yourself where you can compromise. How can you make this a win-win? Some kiddos just don't nap. Perhaps have them do something quiet for a certain amount of time. You could set a timer and say, "We will have a treat or go outside after." (I know, I know. My son would throw the timer at me, so maybe not that.)

Maybe you lay aside your desires and run around with your little ball of energy until your husband comes home and switches with you until bedtime. Maybe he needs preschool, lots of playdates, tot soccer, or a stroller stride class. I'm not saying give in to everything. But I am saying, if you can't beat 'em, then sometimes you should join 'em. This is just a season—an extremely long, hard season, but a season nonetheless. And you will survive because you are strong!

Soon your child will go to school for eight hours a day. It's okay to think that. I know you love them. Then they will come through the door and show you all the things they made and talk about all the things they learned. You can offer them a snack, and soon it will be dinner time! It is as lovely as it sounds, and it will be here before you know it.

As I sit here typing in my office (that I reclaimed after making more bedrooms available upstairs when my girls went to college), my boys, now fourteen and fifteen, leave for school at 7:15 a.m. and don't return until after 5:00 p.m. (even later if they have team sports to attend). I try to make the most of the time they are gone, so I can make the most of the few short hours a day we are together.

This is a season that you will not only get through but, if you let God do a work in your heart regarding control, frustration, expectations, and stubborn standoffs, become a better person for it. Let go of the need to fight every battle and die on every hill. Trust God. Let him transform you into a version of yourself that you are proud of and watch your environment change as well.

I eventually chose not to die on the hill of the dinner table and learned not to fret about mandatory naps. Every day will present you with its own unique set of stubborn standoffs, and you'll need to ask yourself a few questions:

Which battles need to be fought?

Which hills am I willing to die on?

Why does this matter to me?

Does it matter in the long run?

Is it worth the energy it takes and the drama it will create to fight?

What is my ultimate goal?

The fact that your toddler won't nap or stay in his bed or eat his chicken is upsetting at the moment, but does it matter in the grand scheme of things? I mean, surely, we can't have people running amuck, malnourished, and sleep-deprived, right? Right. If your goal is raising happy, healthy children and pointing them to Christ, then sometimes creating peace in your home is an admirable goal as well. "Blessed are the peacemakers..." (Matt. 5:9) You've not gone soft!

We don't want to be like the family in the movie, *Mommy Dearest,* where the steak was left at the dinner table night after night until the daughter would agree to eat it. Finally, maggots grew all over it, and the daughter won! Maybe she just didn't like steak. That's okay.

Try making things they like at dinnertime. Try finding quiet activities to do together at nap time. My son loved Legos and finger painting. When he was old enough, he would read board books to himself in the quiet house while I folded laundry nearby. He felt like he wasn't napping, and I was okay with that.

What is your goal? To be right? To be in control? To say, "Aha! I made you obey." To this day, I will cook what I know most of the family likes to eat and then add a plate of raw veggies or a fruit salad on the side. Anyone is welcomed to make a sandwich if they like. It just won't be me. Is it a big deal to you because you have a strong conviction about nutrition, sleep cycles, or fashion?

For years my son, Adam, would not wear jeans or any pants with buttons or zippers. He claimed they were "scratchy!" He even had a whole phase where he wouldn't wear underwear. I would lay out his clothes downstairs in my office the night before where he liked to get dressed (before it became David's bedroom). It was a lovely system, until one day when I was cleaning and found five pairs of clean underwear stuffed behind the curtain. That *was* a battle I chose to pick (if you were wondering).

When I think about all the standoffs I've had, I realize we truly can't control anyone but ourselves. The sooner we realize that, the better. If they don't want to take a nap, they aren't going to! If they don't want to eat Brussels sprouts, they aren't going to. And if they don't want to put on underwear, girlfriend, they aren't going to.

Everything doesn't have to be hard. Parenting is hard enough. It's okay to take the path of least resistance when you can. It doesn't make you a bad mom. You aren't weak or soft, and you aren't defeated. It makes you selective and wise and, frankly, preserves your sanity.

10

BECOMING MERCIFUL

Can I be honest? I have, at times, yelled, and even swore when angry. I joke about it sometimes but I am not proud. In those moments, I sound like a boiled-over, whistling teapot. I try hard to put the word of God deep down in my soul so that, when I am frustrated and mad, God's words overflow and not my own, but I often fall short because, well, I am a work in progress in need of God's grace and mercy.

I worried my shortcomings would show up in the lives of my children, coming back to bite me like a sassy little mina bird. (I can just hear it now). I was sure at any moment I would get a call from the school saying someone had been using spicy language in the classroom, or been unkind on the playground, and I would have to humble myself yet again. I prayed often for grace and mercy.

It happens to the best of us, right? We have bad days, even bad weeks, and we come home from work edgy and impatient. We say and do things we regret. As adults we say, "I'm sorry, I've just had a hard day" or "I've had it up to here and my patience is wearing thin!" We give each other space, apologize, and even forgive poor behavior and explosive outbursts.

Why is it, then, when our children have bad days we fail to account for it? Perhaps, we even fail to see it. We don't ask them how their day was in the same way we ask other adults. And we don't apply grace and mercy to their situation the way we do for each other. In a sense we end up holding our children to a higher standard, expecting them to behave and obey despite their circumstances or emotions. What a tall order for a child to fill.

After a particularly challenging school week, my son was unprecedentedly mean to me one day after school. We both used spicy words, it got ugly, and I banished him to his room until his daddy came home. At first it felt good to be alone and in a bad mood. Do you know the feeling? I felt justified, all puffed up and talking to myself while my blood pressure boiled over. Maybe my son felt the same.

It's wise to take time to cool off after an argument, though I am careful not to isolate my children too much or for too long as the enemy likes us alone with our thoughts, and the outcome is never good for anyone. It is a delicate balance that I ask the Holy Spirit to help me with.

When my husband arrived, I pleaded my case and shared the whole story (okay, maybe not the *whole* story), and he promptly headed upstairs. I braced myself for more spicy words but, alas, I heard none—no harsh words, no punishment, no stomping or crying. He just asked questions and listened. I'm so thankful for my husband and his calm, wise ways. He knows what this family needs right when we need it.

Soon my son and his dad seriously and calmly descended the staircase and entered the kitchen. My son specifically apologized for the long list of things he had done and said that afternoon, and he hugged me. The Holy Spirit whispered a gentle reminder in my ear that I needed to apologize too and extend the grace and mercy to my son that God so freely extends to me.

I apologized to my son and hugged him tight. I chose to move on and ask him about his day. Instead of sitting alone in his room, my sweet, strong-willed boy sat on a tall stool in the kitchen telling us about the frustrating week he had and how friends had been unkind.

Then he said to me, "Mom, do you know why I love you? Because you don't stay mad at me. It's like when it's over, it's over. And I know I deserve punishment for the things I said and did, but you are nice to me anyway."

I told him, "It's called mercy, and we all need it sometimes, even me! Especially me! It is what Jesus calls us to do."

Why add insult to injury, prolonging a stressful evening and making a bad day worse? Why not choose grace instead of anger? I mean, does God hold a grudge? Does God stay mad, vent, and unload his anger and wrath because of a bad day? No, God pours out his love, grace, and mercy. The Bible teaches that a "gentle answer turns away wrath." (Proverbs 15:1 NASB)

In a world of so much evil and hate, confusion and chaos, sin and stress, I want to err on the side of love, grace, and mercy—starting inside my home:

> If I have all faith so as to remove mountains but do not have love, I am nothing. Love is patient, love is kind, it is not jealous; love does not brag, it is not arrogant. It does not act disgracefully, it does not seek

its own benefit; it is not provoked, does not keep an account of a wrong suffered, it does not rejoice in unrighteousness, but rejoices with the truth; it keeps every confidence, it believes all things, hopes all things, endures all things. Love never fails. (1 Corinthians 13:2b, 4-8)

We don't always get things right in our home. We are human and a messy work in progress, but one thing we have learned to do is love well and extend mercy often! To forgive quickly so we can move on. Life is too short to hold a grudge. I am thankful the love of God covers our sins and leads us back to each other so he can be glorified in our home.

11

ANGER ISSUES

I remember being a strong-willed teen, though if you ask my parents they will tell you I was "spirited" from early on. I remember being angry when frustrated, or not getting my way. My dad likes to tell the story of when I was four and put my hands on my hips and declared, "You're not the boss of me!" If I were to guess, I would say I was more like my dad in that way.

He was a good, strong, hard-working, blue-collar, manly man with a handlebar mustache who didn't take bull from anyone, including his kids, and we respected him for that. On the weekends he taught karate at the rec center, drove dune buggies, fixed our sprinkler systems, and drank Coors from the tan can. It was the 80s, and if you are imagining a cross between the Marlboro man and Magnum P.I. you're pretty close. My dad led our family well which was no easy task considering our strong wills clashed often and made for a bumpy ride through my teen years.

My attitude caused a rift between my dad and me, I slammed a lot of doors, and often brooded in my room. Most teens go through a season of angry moodiness, and I was among the angriest. I was just hot-tempered in general. Then life events added to it, and I was unpleasant to be around. I always felt misunderstood, frustrated, and consequently, alone. I think one of the enemy's most damaging weapons is to get us alone with our feelings, thinking no one cares or understands. The earlier he can do this, the worse off we are. My anger compounded over time. Broken relationships and poor choices as a young adult fanned the flame until I was a force to be reckoned with. My posture was one of "let me hurt you before you hurt me" (emotionally speaking). I let everyone know not to get too close, or they'd be sorry.

Coming to know Jesus in my twenties softened me. I finally felt safe and understood and loved again. I still had an edge because, although I believe Jesus can set you free in an instant, there is still a lifetime of habitual patterns to walk away from and new ones to embrace. I also think there are just some issues that come to the surface and only get worked out once you are married, and some things that come to the surface once you have kids.

True to form, marriage brought out a lot of issues for me, and I tested the limits of my husband's love. It's one thing to be angry and single, but it's another thing to join your life to someone else and bring all that baggage with you. When I was frustrated at work, disappointed in relationships, or angry at the world in general, I would yell and scream at him as if it was all his fault. Was he going to retreat and misunderstand my emotions like my dad? Was he going to leave me or hurt me as other people had? It breaks my heart to think about how mean I was to him at times. Absolutely none of it was his fault! None of it! It's like he walked into the ring of my emotional battlefield and became my punching bag.

One day as he left for school, I threw a coffee cup at his head out of my own unhappiness and inner turmoil. He swerved, and the cup hit the door, shattering all over our tiny apartment. My sweet husband said nothing and kept on walking. The fear of the Lord came over me as I crawled around on the floor, picking up the big pieces of broken pottery and sweeping up the shattered shards of the morning. What had I done? I could have injured him (or worse) and lost the love of my life in an instant and ruined everything!

Had I ruined everything? *Would* he come back? We had no cell phones then, so I waited the entire day for him to return. When he did, I threw *myself* at him in remorse, and we talked for hours. He wasn't mad or harsh but instead assured me he wasn't going anywhere. He would not retreat or leave, and was in it for the long haul. He loved me no matter what. I wasn't too much for him! No one had ever treated me this way, and his words were a soothing balm to my soul. Over time his unconditional love helped to smooth out my sharp edges and restore what the enemy had sought to shatter in my life and in our marriage.

Raising children will bring out your issues too. Issues you haven't dealt with will come up along with some you thought you've already handled. There's nothing like a defiant toddler to stir up your anger or a disrespectful child to make you feel like a failure in public. My girls were relatively sweet and easy to raise. I mean, they frustrated me at times, and I was worn out from the sheer exhaustion of motherhood, but that felt normal and appropriate and for the most part, never really triggered my temper.

My son was a different story altogether. He would not sleep when I wanted, eat what I wanted, sit when I asked, or hand over whatever contraband he was about to throw over the railing when I asked him for it! He has spit, thrown poop, and said the ever-dreaded "I hate you!" more times than I ever care to hear (to which you must make yourself say, "I'm sorry to hear that, I love you!").

A good friend reminded me "we have to be the adults." It does us no good to stoop to low levels with an angry or defiant child. And it's hard, dare I say, nearly impossible, not to if you are dealing with your own anger issues. It behooves us all to deal with these issues sooner than later. According to Dr. Leon F Seltzer in his Psychology Today article:

> "Anger is tricky in that it is predominantly a secondary emotion whose main function is to safeguard us from primary emotions such as embarrassment, fear, shame, guilt, depression, or grief. Its seductiveness and danger lie in the fact that it is the only negative emotion devoid of any vulnerability. We cling to it in situations where our sense of pride, competence, respect, intelligence, or attractiveness is perceived at risk. For we dodge the ego threatening hardball in furiously hurling it back at our perceived assailant." (That's the let me hurt you before you hurt me part... self-preservation at its finest!)

"Ironically, when we get angry, we're not fighting someone or something, we're fighting ourselves in the sense that we're forcefully pushing back down disturbing feelings that an outside force has brought much too close to our fragile emotional surface."[1]

You are a ticking time bomb ready to blow! This makes perfect sense. I wish I had read this twenty years ago. I also wish I could explain it to my toddler. "See, this is why mommy is so angry.... Her fragile pride is being exposed!"

Parenting is the perfect pot where anger can stew. It is the single most vulnerable setting we will ever be in. Every fragile emotion we have is brought to the surface daily. We are given the choice to find a way to hold it all together or lose it on everyone and wreak havoc on our family.

I didn't want to wreak havoc on my family. And I know you don't want to either. My desire was quite the opposite. I wanted a happy, healthy, thriving family. I wanted to keep my precious relationships intact and not say anything in the heat of the moment I would regret later or, even worse, hurt someone so deeply it couldn't be taken back.

My husband and I decided years ago not to say things like, "I want a divorce!" or "I wish I had never married you!" or even "I hate you!"—no low blows or dirty fighting. The same is true in parenting. Resolve right now to set a high bar for this. I know spending a long day with a strong-willed child can leave you feeling like a ticking time bomb. But I also believe God wants to work that out of you, and he will use your current circumstances to do so.

The Bible says in Proverbs 14:1 that "The wise woman builds her house, but the foolish tears it down with her own hands." Sometimes with her own *words?*

There was a marked shift in my family when I began to ask God to remove this anger from me. I would stop and ask myself, "Why am I so mad, frustrated, angry, and upset?" It seems like the only time I'm not angry is when I have a perfect day. Why is that? Is it because a good day meant I was a good mom, was a success, did something right, or had everything under control? Yeah, me! Look at me! I was actually frustrated at myself for being unable to control the situation and make my children behave. Raging on everyone does nothing but bring more shame and condemnation, creating an atmosphere where anger is expected and people are made to fear you.

You are allowed to be disappointed the day did not go better. Things aren't always going to go your way. Children have a mind and a will of their own, and you cannot control everyone and every situation. You must control your temper. Look at the big picture: there will be good days and bad and neither should dictate your worth. You are showing up, doing the best you can in a tremendously difficult situation.

If you are feeling angry, try removing yourself from the situation for a bit. Tap someone else in (perhaps a spouse, a friend, or a relative). You will be okay! Your kiddos will be okay! You just need someone to keep them alive while you step away for an hour or two. Don't try to be a martyr. It's amazing what a little time away can do for your relationship with your child. You will be a new woman with a new perspective when you return.

If today did not go well, ask yourself why, and start again tomorrow. If you are like me, you are saying, "The day did not go well because my kid is a monster who does not listen!" Ask yourself what *small* thing you could do tomorrow to foster a calmer atmosphere, whether an adjustment in your attitude, a tweak in activities, "tapping out," or offering grace and mercy (instead of an everything-must-be-perfect-or-heads-are-gonna-roll attitude). Try getting an extra hour of sleep or waking up an extra hour early to have an extra cup of coffee to "gird up your loins." Invite Grandma over to help. Maybe what you need is to not invite Grandma over! What does the day need?

Your child might not change, but you just might, and that change may affect him and bring about future change. It's crazy, I know! It works in marriages all the time, so why not try it with our kiddos. Hey, the worst-case scenario is you change, which may make for a more pleasant household. In my experience, when you change and allow God to set you free from your anger issues, you will see a change in those around you as well.

As soon as I realized what was driving my anger, things began to change. I didn't have to be in control of everything. My feisty toddler's behavior was not a reflection of my self-worth. Go easy on yourself and your family. Every day will not be perfect. Celebrate progress.

12

WHEN YOU SEE YOURSELF IN YOUR CHILD

Have you ever noticed the things we say when we see someone's new baby? We say things like, "Oh look, he has his daddy's eyes and his mommy's smile," or "Ya know, I think he looks just like Aunt Sarah." Maybe there is a redhead in a family of brunettes or an outgoing "chatty Cathy" in a family of introverts. Every once in a while, we find ourselves saying, "Where in the world did *that* behavior come from?"

Chances are that your little apple did not fall far from the family tree, and you don't have to look far to see similarities. I often see my husband and myself in our children. They are tall and athletic with thick, blond hair. They are also super smart, funny, kind-hearted, compassionate, creative, and loyal (yep, that sounds like us all right)—end of story.

Quite the contrary! Sometimes I recognize things in my children I don't like. Their wills are so strong it can be an exhausting task trying to parent them. They can be stubborn, bossy, and mean-spirited towards one another. And, well, some of them, in particular, can be downright explosive when angered! Hmmm, maybe *that* sounds more like us.

When I see my children angry to the point of rage, I feel sympathetic because I can relate. I know they don't like being that way, and my heart longs to help them. The Bible gives some great insight into exactly how to help. It's not what you might think.

"How can you say to your brother, 'Let me take the speck out of your eye,' when all the time there is a plank in your own eye? You hypocrite, first take the plank out of your own eye, and then you will see clearly to remove the speck out of your brother's eye." (Matt. 7:5)

Simply put, we should take a look at ourselves and see if the behavior we see in our children might lie in us. If so, seek to fix it within ourselves first. This shows our children there is hope for them as we find victory, not only giving them something to emulate, but free to find victory as well. It's a plank in my eye, but just a speck in my kiddo? This is good news! The hard part is over. There's just a sliver to remove for my child. This I can do!

There is a level of mercy and compassion that comes from personally walking out of something and then reaching back to help someone else, especially your strong-willed child. You can say, "I know, baby, this is hard. But I've been there. If I can do it, you can do it! Let me show you how."

I am writing from the airplane today on an early morning flight. I am traveling home with my tired family from our Christmas vacation in California. So much fun was had and so many memories made, but now my silent crew shuffled methodically and robotically single file down the aisle to sit down, three seats on the right and three seats on the left.

The trips home are always uneventful. Everyone has headphones on or their noses in a book, paying no attention to the flight attendant and her safety instructions, except for me. I close my laptop to listen. I always listen. I figure the one time I don't will be the one time I need to. Plus, it feels rude to ignore her. So I smile, nod, and politely listen.

The instructions are as follows: put on *your* oxygen mask first, and *then* assist your child. I have heard these instructions a hundred times before, but today it dawned on me just how profound they are. I am of no help to my child if I am not healthy physically *or emotionally!* If I can get healthy and free, I can show my child how to overcome it as well.

I imagined, God forbid, the oxygen mask falling from the compartment overhead. How might I show my children exactly what to do while calming them down and reassuring them everything would be okay? "See, watch me. Look at me. We will get through this! You're doing great! See how I'm doing it? Do it just like this, and you'll be okay!" It might not go exactly like that but as *you* get victory over *your* bad habit patterns and struggles, you can begin to model that for your child.

When I am angry and yell, my children get angry and yell. As I begin to change, soften, and give grace, I see a change occur in my family. If it doesn't happen immediately, I have patience and celebrate the small victories in me and them. I praise them along the way, recognizing and acknowledging their strengths.

For the few struggles your child has, I bet there are a million strengths. Be sure and point them out often and try to help them flourish. We often give the negative too much attention and forget to acknowledge God-given strengths and celebrate God-given victories. It can be discouraging working through a tough time. Encouragement, praise, patience, and grace go a long way.

Remember to pray. When dealing with a difficult child or a child going through a challenging time, I remind myself this is the child I prayed for. In the dark hours, when I thought God had forgotten about me, when other babies died in my womb, when the doctors said another baby was unlikely, I heard God say, "Believe for a son!" This child was the answer. I fought for him then and I will fight for him now. I am sure you have a place in your heart like this, a story, an ache—especially regarding the child you see yourself in the most. Let love and passion press you forward into a healthy relationship and victory for the whole family.

I believe these patterns we see are hereditary. They are often referred to as generational strongholds and can be broken by allowing God to change *you*. This in turn empowers you to help your child do the same. Remember, your family is like a garden; weed and pluck out that which does not belong. Get rid of the things that have crept in over time that seek to choke out the good that should be growing—like love, joy, peace, patience, kindness, goodness, faithfulness, gentleness, and self-control. Cry out to God. Be honest with him. Ask him to show you how to bring about permanent, life-altering, generational change for you, your children, and even your children's children!

PART 4

FROM TANTRUMS TO TRANSFORMATION

Fathers, do not exasperate your children; instead, bring them up in the training and instruction of the Lord.

Ephesians 6:4

13

WHICH WAY SHOULD WE GO?

Well, friend, here it is! This section is all about discipline. Perhaps the book will just naturally fall open to this section for you, or if you are like me when I get my hands on a new parenting book, you might flip right to the section on discipline. It's human nature to want concrete solutions and answers to the things we struggle with the most. I know just how real the struggle with discipline can be, so let's talk all about it.

The desperate desire to succeed at motherhood can cause us to try just about any suggested method of discipline. The yearning to have our children obey and be good can even lead us to compromise our conscience. I am guilty of trying things that I knew in my heart weren't going to work for my family. When there was no change in behavior or things became worse, I would wonder what was wrong with me. Why was I such a failure?

Let me be the first to tell you (if you don't already know) that your child's behavior is not a reflection of your self-worth. Nothing is wrong with your child either. He or she is simply strong-willed, which is a good thing. Remember? But we tend to fall into the negative thought pattern of thinking something is either wrong with us or wrong with them:

"I will *make* this work if it's the last thing I do!"

"I will see your strong will and raise you mine!"

We lose our ever-loving minds in the name of "You are going to obey me no matter what!"

"The stronger *your* will is, the stronger *mine* will be, buddy!"

"Do not try me today!"

It takes a strong-willed mama to raise a strong-willed child. This is true, but how you channel that will is the key. I found a calmer, healthier path and allowed God to not only transform my outlook on discipline but transform me and my relationship with my children. Let's take a look at some things that worked for me and some things that didn't.

Trying to make a strong-willed child obey can be a near-impossible task. They will throw a tantrum of grand proportions right there in the store or in the foyer of church or while you are trying to interview for a new private school. They will even throw it at the volleyball game where you told them to sit quietly.

"Why won't you just sit quietly?" I asked my son.

To which he replied, "I won't sit quietly because I hate dumb, stupid volleyball games!"

My girlfriend and I still laugh about that to this day and refer to them as "dumb, stupid volleyball games." He wasn't going to do what he did not want to do.

You can exercise *your* strong will all you want, but just know that sometimes the will of a child has no ceiling, and it will be a messy battle that you will lose if you are not careful. *My* fleshly strong will wanted to slap him into the next court (not recommended) or take him to the bathroom and spank him (probably making things worse and causing me to miss the whole game). It's better in these circumstances to be as the Bible says: "Wise as a serpent and harmless as a dove." (Matt. 10:16 NKJV) It's what a mature strong will looks like—harnessed, tempered, even bridled. There are better options than dragging him off by his arm to teach him a thing or two. There is always a calmer, wiser option. Look for it.

Honestly, I could have just swallowed my pride and laughed it off, done nothing, or dealt with it later in private. All very good options. But what would onlookers say to each other? Onlookers will say what they will say. Pay zero attention! They will come and go in this life, but this is your family, not theirs. You do what you've got to do. They don't go home with your child—you do. You want to be proud of yourself when you lay your head on your pillow at night. You want to hear God say, "Well done, good and faithful servant." What does that look like for you?

I could have hired a babysitter or only gone to the games where my husband could help. Chad and I could have switched off staying home with the boys. (Which we eventually did and then a rumor spread that we were divorced.) Pay—zero—attention! Maybe I should've had the forethought to get them good and tired beforehand and then given them snacks and iPads. This probably would have backfired on me because sometimes being too tired is a problem for them as well, and I would inevitably incur harsh judgment from someone for screen time allowance.

I have done all of this at various times, and what I want you to know is this:

- There is no one way. There is just what works for you. Find it and be consistent.

- Pray for discernment.

- The will of a child can have no ceiling, and it's okay to make a choice that de-escalates the situation for all.

- Slow and steady wins the race.

- Remember—just like dumb, stupid volleyball—this is a season. It will be over eventually. You will survive and so will your child.

My husband commented just the other day on how different our lives have become. We used to white-knuckle our way through certain seasons of parenting with dread (volleyball season to mention one). But now with our daughters in college, we roll up to the boys' high school games without a care in the world except where to eat afterward. It is a well-earned privilege. Be encouraged. You'll get there. I promise.

Friend, sometimes the victory is in the slow and steady, day-by-day. How did I ask for guidance and strength to yield my own strong will to God in the moment? I have often stopped on the spot and said out loud, "Lord Jesus, come now and help me in this situation! Give me patience and guidance and self-control. Lower my heart rate, Lord. Help me think rationally and make wise decisions that please you. Amen." And I look for him to answer. I suppose it's a more elaborate and spiritual version of counting to ten. It has been my saving grace.

I am acutely aware that my children may get their strong will from me, so I have learned to empathize with their struggle. It's hard enough as an adult. I can only imagine how hard it is to be little and strong-willed—angry, frustrated, and unable to find the words to convey strong emotions. I recognize the importance of modeling this to help *them* overcome the temptations that I know too well. Again, I stop and pray, "Lord, how do you want to use my strong will to train and discipline my child? Help me help them." It's in this cry for help, this surrendering of my will, where I find strength.

I have learned, through much trial and error, to stop and ask myself what God wants me to do in each situation. Is what I'm currently doing glorifying him, and is it pointing my child to Christ? It helps to turn to the Word of God for clarity. The Bible has a lot to say about the subject of discipline. Specifically, that it is necessary and for our own good. It also says that parents who love their children discipline them. But what exactly does that mean? Isn't discipline just a nice term for spanking? Is there a difference? They are different words with different meanings. Discipline is actually a broader term than just spanking as punishment. I love this quote from Rick Warren:

> "The attitude behind punishment is anger. The attitude behind discipline is love....God doesn't want you to punish your kids. He wants you to discipline

them. When you correct in anger, it always produces one thing: resentment. What God says to do is to correct while looking toward the future, making sure the mistake won't be repeated. Focusing on the future is redemptive, not destructive."[1]

I wish I had read that quote years ago. It is such a good reminder to focus on the future and not the quick fix. So often we want results, and we want them now! We are so desperate that we'll try anything. Our tendency can be to think, *This isn't working!* We throw it out too soon and hastily try something else. I tend to do this when I diet. (I hear my husband saying, "Well, you only tried it for two weeks!") Let me try something else, then something else, then another fad. This happens until my body is so confused, and my metabolism is shot. If I had just done the consistent, healthy, long-term thing (that I knew was best for me), I'd be much further along. Remember—it's a marathon, not a sprint. Slow and steady wins the race.

My husband calls the process healthy discipline with time and constant pressure. Healthy discipline applied consistently over a long period will yield positive results. I am talking about eighteen years of consistent love and patience, while redirecting conversations, modeling, teaching, and, yes, *healthy discipline.* When my children leave my home, our values will be ingrained in their spirit, not from harsh punishment but from loving, consistent discipline. Then the wisdom that we've deposited over the years will be readily available in their spirit when they need it.

A game-changer for me was when I began to discipline out of love instead of punishing out of anger. I truly want the best for my children. I want to help them succeed and grow, not resent me! When I began to understand my children and their unique needs and personalities, I could see better how to lovingly help each of them overcome the challenges they faced (or as the Bible describes "the sin that so easily entangles them"). (Heb. 12:1)

All children need rules to follow and consequences to reap that vary depending on the age of the child and the severity of the offense. They might lose money, possessions, or privileges. They might have to do some extra chores or have bedtime moved up. And, of course, good behavior is always rewarded. I call it finding their currency. What gets their attention? In my house, simply turn the Wi-Fi off, and everyone comes running. Everyone's household will look different, but what we can't do is not discipline our children. We can't shirk our responsibility to "train them up" as the Bible says. Consistency is key. What is God saying to you, and what does that look like carried out in your family?

There is powerful confidence in knowing what works and doesn't work for you. Avoid trying to please the public. Get to know your child so intimately that you could say, "I can see how that idea would work for some families, but that probably won't be the best for mine." That's empowering! Then begin to find those things that bear fruit and bring life, confidence and transformation to your family.

14

MISTAKES: I'VE MADE A FEW

I just got off the phone with a dear friend who is struggling with her lively little ones. She said, "Tell me what to do! Give me practical and tangible things to do!"

"I wish it were that simple," I said. "Honestly, tell me what you are currently doing, and we can brainstorm together. I will be your super nanny for the day. I'll tell you what worked for me and what didn't. But keep in mind that your family is different from mine, and every child responds differently." As you read all the good books and listen to wise advice, pray and lean into the Holy Spirit. You do what works best for your family. It takes knowing your child thoroughly, and it takes time. I know no one wants to hear this, but it's the truth.

Find your sweet spot with each child. Try, and try again, and try some more. Resist the inclination to give way to anger. Resist the temptation to throw in the towel. Stay in the ring with your child, and fight the good fight of faith! Celebrate small victories when you see them. Walk in faith, grace, mercy, and love. This is what I have done over the years. I've stayed in the ring, clung to Jesus, cried out to God, and listened for his voice.

I've had a lot of success! I've also made a lot of mistakes looking for that quick fix of behavior modification. I've said, "Tell me what to do, and I'll do it!" I have tried everything! Most of which, sadly, did not bear lasting fruit or point my children to Christ. "Like what?" you ask.

Let's pretend we are sitting at my kitchen table brainstorming over coffee. Let's discuss for a moment what didn't work for me, and then we can move on to what did.

Time-outs worked well for some but not for others. I have a love-hate relationship with time-outs. When my girls were little, if they were sent to their rooms for a time-out, they would go and think about what they did. They would often write a sweet note of apology, and there would be forgiveness and reconciliation. Even to this day, when my youngest son, David (fourteen years old), is sent to his room, he will fall asleep almost immediately, letting us know that being tired is most of his problem.

But Adam never stayed in his room. The back and forth of it all overshadowed whatever small infraction sent him there in the first place. Except for the one time, he flew a paper airplane down the stairs. On it he had written, "Do you forgive me? Check Yes or No!" (Ugh, that kid! Pro tip: Always check "Yes!")

From a very young age, Adam would come out of his room so many times it was exhausting and not a worthy investment of my time. There was a season where, instead of going to his room, my son would defiantly run outside to the backyard. Out of my frustration and desperation, I would lock the back door. I would not let him in until he calmed down or agreed to go to his room. Again, these are my mistakes. Please learn from them, but don't feel too sorry for him as there was a swimming pool, outdoor kitchen, flat-screen TV, couches, and a fridge (not to mention a basketball hoop) a few yards away.

When I would look away to tend to my one million other children (that's how it seems sometimes), instead of making himself comfortable, Adam would push anything and everything into the pool in an attempt to get my attention. Have you ever tried to recover an upside-down patio umbrella from the bottom of a pool? It weighs approximately fifty-five tons! I would end up letting him inside because nothing seemed to work. Who remembers why he was in time-out in the first place? To my point, time-outs weren't the best option with my strongest-willed son. I know that now! In hindsight, I should have found a different method of discipline for him.

Chores can feel like a chore for you. Doling out chores is an age-old and seemingly straightforward form of punishment for disobedience: rake the leaves, mow the lawn, do the dishes. (You know the drill.) But for my family and me, it just produced too many conflicts. I would spend so much time instructing the children (especially when they were little) on how to do chores properly or even doing the chores with them that, honestly, I should have just done them myself and taught them at a later date. Then they could incorporate chores into their lives as a positive part of their daily routine.

It never sat well with me that I was doing chores alongside my child, spending what might look like quality time with "the offender." Meanwhile, the rest of the children sat around waiting to spend time with me or start whatever family plans we had for the weekend. It felt like the *siblings* were being punished. There is a time and a place to teach children that their actions affect those around them, but this didn't seem like the proper setting to me. Chores didn't seem like the right discipline tool for me, at least not when they were little.

Tough love for little ones is not always logical. When my kids were in elementary school, I read the popular book *Parenting with Love and Logic* by Foster Cline and Jim Fay.[2] Some principles in it and the companion book *Love and Logic Magic for Early Childhood*[3] were especially helpful. The author, however, describes a scenario where he made his elementary-age kids get out of the car for fighting and made them walk home. I believe he circled back around his sleepy little cul-de-sac to follow them safely and slowly, and there seemed to be a lot of calm planning involved. I could stop right here and take a hard pass.

I have attempted this strategy on the drive home from *our* children's elementary school. We live a mile and a half from the school. It's too far to walk at dawn or in the fog or in one-hundred-degree heat or *when you are five years old* and too close for a bus. The fights, the sass, and the stress that can occur in a three-minute trip to or from school are unbelievable. (My goodness!) I have once or twice abruptly invited them to get out and walk. I quickly regretted it. They were too young, and it did not seem safe.

I did, however, stop the car and ask my now 14-year-old son to walk himself home just the other day. We were three houses from home, and he was being irrationally moody and I had had enough. I invited him to get out and walk the rest of the way. He was so angry that he said, "This isn't solving anything!"

To which I replied, "Oh yes, it is. Bye-bye! See you in a minute." Then I drove myself peacefully into the driveway. *This* made safe sense to me. But when they were little, I would refrain. When they are little and this is used as punishment or a teaching tool, I don't think it brings about lasting change. It doesn't seem safe and certainly does not point them to Jesus.

Maybe my children thought, "Dang! Mom is not playing today. We'd better shape up or she won't drive us again." Maybe. Or maybe they were just scared (which is not good at all!) The fact is that I would indeed drive them to school again for their safety, and the lesson could be learned differently. This is not discipline! This does not have the long view in mind. This was me reacting out of anger and frustration and blowing off steam.

I suggest you bite the bullet, get them safely home, and then calmly talk about consequences for poor behavior in the car. You could try things like planning to have them walk to school next time until they can agree to behave in the car (again, depending on age, maturity, and safety concerns). You could push back bedtime, take away a privilege, or restrict them from a toy or a favorite show. The good news is you have plenty of sensible options.

I know it is tempting to react and get a quick fix. But try thinking about how this can be a lesson in character and point your child to Christ. (And, of course, safety first!) A wonderful book that I highly recommend that presents consequences and focuses on following Christ is *Loving Your Kids on Purpose* by Danny Silk.

A bad taste in their mouth is a bad idea! Strong-willed children can often use strong words to convey their strong emotions. Let's be honest, so can strong mamas! There were times when my children were particularly sassy or mouthy. You know those times when you step back and think, *Excuse me! Who do you think you are with your hands on your hips and your tongue wagging at me like that?*

I had a friend tell me I ought to put hot sauce on my son's tongue when he gets sassy. (I guess it's the modern-day version of soap-in-the-mouth—which I also tried. Ugh, I know!) I called her back and said, "Well, now I have a fire-breathing dragon on my hands!" The soap produced a similar scenario to a bubble-making machine. (No lie!) Perhaps in my friend's case, it shocked sense into her kiddo, stopped him in his tracks, and made him think twice about being sassy ever again. Hooray for them!

My son stared me right in the eyes, licked his lips, and said, "Yummy!" (I had to put myself in a timeout after that one!) Again, the long-term desire for me is to capture the hearts of my children which I hope will lead to behavior modification. We train, teach, model, and reinforce always with the intent to capture the heart and point them to Jesus.

The best advice I have for a sassy mouth is to create a gentler environment. Continue to write the script. Speak the language and narrative that you want to foster in your home. I would sometimes make a bitter disapproving face when foul or harsh language was used in my home like *I* had soap in *my* mouth. They would get the hint that that language or behavior is not pleasing or acceptable. Or they would go out into the world and realize it. They would catch on eventually.

Show your children with your own words and actions what is right and what is wrong. Model for them how to treat people. They are growing and learning, fighting outside influences, hormones, a desire for independence, and strong wills that wage war on them all day long, every minute of every day. There is a proverbial angel on one shoulder and devil on the other vying for their attention, their affections—their souls!

The message regarding your values, standards, and love that you present to them in your home will play on repeat in their minds and spirits as they get older if you are consistent. I know this now. But, boy, did I try everything. I wanted something to work. I wanted behavior modification. I wanted them to obey! It seemed like the ultimate goal at the time, but there is a higher goal that takes time and patience and perseverance.

This is where it becomes a marathon, not a sprint. This is when you realize that it is not about control but consistency. Remember, you need time and constant pressure. Find that sweet spot that works for your family, bears fruit, and pleases God. And do it consistently for a long time. Now, let's talk about spanking!

15

MY WRESTLING MATCH
WITH SPANKING

Growing up, I do not remember ever getting spanked. In fact, I specifically remember not being spanked. I remember a time when my dad tried to spank me once for something I'm sure was deserving of discipline. I hid behind a door, pushing against it with my feet. He was angry on the other side. He was trying to come in with my mom behind him, begging him not to do whatever it was he was planning to do when he got his hands on me!

My dad never did put his hands on me but when he was mad, he would take off his belt and snap it really loud, and my brother and I would run as fast as we could to our rooms. There was also a lot of counting to three, and a lot of running. I'm not sure what we were running from, but we ran. That was kind of how it went in my house. When we were older, we were sent to our rooms to cool off. We always apologized, and we were always back to being a family again.

I remember the only time my mom spanked my older brother. He had called some girl a bad name (that rhymes with ditch) on the way home from school. Her mom came to our house to tell my mom. I guess she didn't have our phone number or something. (It truly was the

70s. Nowadays, I get Facebook messages from other moms about my child's behavior.)

I was young, but I still remember her standing in our doorway with her daughter, demanding recompense. My mom was young too. The woman was mad and told my mom that my brother needed a "good spanking." When my mom retells the story now, she says, "I did not want to spank him but felt the pressure. Besides, that woman was—well—being a 'ditch' too!" We all laugh about it now. I am sure there are things our children are doing that mortify us now that we will laugh about someday.

These were my only encounters with spanking until I was much older. The local church I attended in college was very family-oriented. I learned a lot about early childhood parenting practices as I noticed that most families in my church seemed to have extremely polite and obedient children. They also believed that spanking was biblical. Everyone seemed to fall into the same camp with a "spare the rod spoil the child" theology, and I learned that spanking was a widely held belief system in the Christian culture. According to a study in the Huffington Post:

> Recent polls indicate that up to 70% of Americans, both Black and White, approve of some form of corporal punishment of children—with Evangelical Christians coming in at over 85%. Spanking in one form or another is as American as apple pie—and the practice is deeply rooted in, and most often defended by, a reading of traditional translations of the English Bible.[4]

Scriptures in question include:

- Proverbs 13:24: Whoever spares the rod hates their children, but the one who loves their children is careful to discipline them.

- Proverbs 19:18: Discipline your children, for in that there is hope; do not be a willing party to their death.

- Proverbs 22:15: Folly is bound up in the heart of a child, but the rod of discipline will drive it far away.

- Proverbs 23:13-14: Do not withhold discipline from a child; if you punish them with the rod, they will not die. Punish them with the rod and save them from death.

- Proverbs 29:15: A rod and a reprimand impart wisdom, but a child left undisciplined disgraces its mother.

As a young mom, I wanted to do the right thing. I wanted to be a good Christian mama. I read so many early parenting books advocating spanking and using scripture like the ones from this article to back it up. When my girls were little, we were big spankers. We would swat their hand for grabbing things off the table or throwing food or pulling hair. We would spank them on the bottom with any spanking tool deemed a worthy "rod." Swats on the butt were doled out for disobedience and rebellion or tantrums. Then we would prayerfully restore them and talk about what was wrong and how to ask God for forgiveness.

Well, that was the plan, anyway. For the most part, we stuck to it, and it seemed somewhat effective. I mean who knows? My girls are fabulous, grown adults now and, may I say, pretty well-adjusted. But they never really gave me much trouble over the years and were pretty compliant in general. Honestly, who wants to get swatted on the butt? So it made me think spanking must have been successful.

But in the back of my mind, I doubted. Is this working, and is this the best form of discipline? In hindsight, I wonder if, given love and firm boundaries, they wouldn't have just grown out of a lot of it. It's something I ponder often. People would tell me that spanking was okay as long as it was done in love and with self-control, prayer, and restoration of your child. Yeah, okay. Who is doing that all the time? Seriously, who?

Admittedly, I have a temper, a situational temper, a sleep-deprived, desperate-for-order-and-peace temper. Combine that with a strong-willed child, and you have a very volatile situation on your hands.

I am not saying you should spank, and I am not saying you shouldn't. You know your family, and you know your temperament and theirs. I will tell you that my youngest son, David, would straighten up and apologize, cry, and become remorseful at the mention of a spanking. (Even writing that makes me a little sad.) But Adam was another story.

It was as if Adam's will was beyond the effects of spanking. It never brought about remorse. It never made the behavior stop. Depending on the day, it either angered him or me or both. Dr. James Dobson warns us in his book *The New Strong-Willed Child-surviving birth through adolescence,* putting a toddler over your knee only works for a few years at best.[5] Making him hold still for a spanking was a preposterously insane idea in my house.

Not even as a toddler would my son hold still. He would buck like a wild bucking bronco, and someone would end up getting hurt. One time, as he was getting older, he bucked off my lap so hard, he hit his head on the nearby dresser and got the hugest black eye. It seemed to make him madder, and that frustrated me more. I had fun explaining that to the preschool teacher.

It became more than just swats on the bottom and restorative prayers. Doors were slammed, and toys were thrown. Well-meaning friends would tell me, "His will is strong, and you need to break it. Spank him more and harder. Be consistent, and don't back down!" I wanted to invite them into my home to see the turmoil, chaos, and unrest that it was creating. Not to mention the other children waiting to do homework, have dinner, or be tucked in. In a way, I could see the dance that my son would engage me in. From a very young age, perhaps not even consciously, he had all of my attention, even though it was negative, and his siblings did not. The irony was not lost on me.

Adam would disobey and then run away to his room or be sent there. Then he would run out and throw toys over the railing until one of us came to deal with him. Then he would hide under the bed, and I would pull him out to try to spank him. His long, wiry body and lanky legs were almost stronger than I was. I was attempting to spank him out of anger, and even rage. It didn't start that way but gone were the days I could pretend this was a calm, "biblical," restorative experience.

I would even sit on him, positioned on his legs with my elbow in his back in order to spank his bottom. He would buck and flip and kick. Sometimes I would "win," and sometimes I would lose. I remember one particular evening. (I'm not even sure what Adam did.) We both sat there on the floor of his room, all torn apart now, partly from the tantrum he threw when he was sent there and partly from me trying to catch him. We were both a hot, sweaty mess, and I think we can all agree that there were no winners here.

I thought to myself, "This right here is not okay and can't possibly please God. This feels more like child abuse to me. I looked at my son breathing heavily in the corner of his room, confused and frustrated and not backing down, and I decided I needed to find a better way.

Listen, I love God, and I love his Word and desire to follow his ways. If I could have made sense of this all, and it was bearing fruit, then I might be singing a different tune. Perhaps loving, controlled, and restorative spanking has worked for you. (Hooray if it has!) But I suspect not if you find yourself here.

The whole spanking thing began not to sit well with me. It didn't seem to be "driving out foolishness" as the Bible says. (Pr. 22:15) I mean, maybe it was, in the sense that my child might have thought, *Ouch, that hurt! Now you've got my attention!* or *I didn't like that, so I'll try to obey!* It is similar to how getting a traffic ticket gets your attention and "drives out foolishness." You think, *Okay! Okay!. I've learned my lesson!* But to me, it didn't feel like my child was learning a lesson. It felt more like I was venting my anger on my son. Even Dobson has tight parameters around his loose recommendations regarding spanking. He doesn't recommend spanking a child under the age of eighteen months and says that by age three to five you should phase spanking out. He suggests never spanking an adolescent and always having other methods in your parenting repertoire.[6]

Even if we see a clear biblical mandate regarding spanking as we know it, there is a small window of appropriateness and effectiveness. This leads me to believe we should explore other options as well. It can kind of make your head spin trying to figure it out. In the meantime, your child's behavior is still the elephant in the room. Here's what I do know. Child abuse is not good parenting. The Bible has a lot to say about what good parenting looks like.

- Psalm 127: 3-5: "Children are a heritage from the LORD, offspring a reward from him. Like arrows in the hands of a warrior are children born in one's youth. Blessed is the man whose quiver is full of them.

- Romans 12:17-18: "Do not repay anyone evil for evil. Be careful to do what is right in the eyes of everyone. If it is possible as far as it depends on you, live at peace with everyone."

- Proverbs 22:6: "Start children off on the way they should go, and even when they are old, they will not turn from it."

- Colossians 3:21: "Fathers, do not embitter your children, or they will become discouraged."

- Ephesians 6:4: "Fathers, do not exasperate your children; instead, bring them up in the training and instruction of the Lord."

- Proverbs 29:17: "Discipline your children, and they will give you peace; they will bring you the delights you desire."

- Proverbs 1:8-9: "Listen, my son, to your father's instruction and do not forsake your mother's teaching. They are a garland to grace your head and a chain to adorn your neck."

- Deuteronomy 6:7: "Impress them on your children. Talk about them when you sit at home and when you walk along the road, when you lie down and when you get up.

- 3 John 1:4: I have no greater joy than to hear that my children are walking in the truth.

For me, spanking was not the ultimate magic method of discipline, and I needed to find what worked for my child. This particular method did not work for me and this particular child, and that is okay. If no one has ever given you permission not to spank, let me be the first. It's okay to find a different way.

16

ARE WE HAVING FUN YET?

I had never written this story down before now. I have told it to a few friends, but writing it down felt a bit like reliving it. I just wasn't ready for that. But here I am, writing it down and talking about it with you. It was the day my son ran away, and I chased him. He'd run away before but never on vacation, and never before did I chase him—well, not like this. It was one of the hardest and scariest parenting moments in my life, a moment where I felt like I used up all of my strength and energy as well as all of God's strength and energy too. It was a defining moment in my parenting journey and my walk with God.

When my children were little, we didn't attempt much travel or plan big family vacations. I knew some people who did, and I always marveled at them. I also wondered if it was actually as fun as they claimed, or if it was more work than they let on. But then again, every family is different. What works for one doesn't always work for another. Who am I to say? But it felt similar to knowing not to gather everyone for a fancy family picture in the bluebonnets. I just knew our limits. It's good to know your limits and those of your children.

Once the girls were old enough to carry their luggage and the boys were about three and four, we thought we'd try our hand at a vacation. For a few summers in a row, we traveled back to California where my husband and I both grew up and all the grandparents still lived. We would fly to Northern California to see Chad's parents for the Fourth of July and then drive seven hours to Southern California to see my family after that.

We had a great time once we finally got there, decorating Papa Bill's golf cart for the community parade and going to the early morning pancake breakfast in their sleepy, little neighborhood. One year down at the beach, my dad brought fishing poles and taught the boys how to fish off the back patio of our rented beach house at high tide. They caught three small sand sharks and a leopard shark. It was so exciting!

It was *getting* to California that was a chore. Adam did not travel well, especially in a car. His mood would range anywhere from your normal cranky toddler to a crazed maniac we had trapped in a straitjacket. He would yell, "If you people don't let me out of this car right now, I am gonna jump out and run back to Texas!" He was exhausting, always contrary, always difficult, and always yelling. Trying to make six people happy in a minivan that at moments felt like a tiny clown car was no easy task. I, too, had thoughts of "jumping out and running back to Texas!"

Family vacations are just hard. Especially when kids are little. My friend Suzanne describes it as trying to live your regular life but in someone else's house without your own stuff. Oh, how I understand that! One of my *biggest* struggles is trying to visit with relatives and friends at the expense of time with my children.

I wonder who else gets this dynamic. It's like when someone keeps talking when your baby is crying or your toddler is pulling things off the counter. You are trying not to seem distracted, but you are. And they aren't picking up on your non-verbal cues, or they don't care. Or it's similar to walking a rambunctious dog when someone stops you and wants to talk. You get the leash all tangled around your legs, and your dog poops on the sidewalk. If they would have just let you keep on truckin', waving casually from afar, things would have gone smoothly, and you could have played off the fact that you had a rambunctious, crazy dog. You could have appeared normal for a moment or at least until you got back to your house. This right here is the headspace that I live in daily, and it is magnified when on vacation.

Every year, I would come home saying, "That was fun!" but thinking, *Not really. I mean, I love the beach, and I love my family, but, sheesh, I'm exhausted!* So we continue to visit this particular stretch of the coast where our backyard is the sand. Everyone loves it! (Well, most of us. Mostly just me, honestly.)

My whole vacation could seriously just be spent laying on the beach, but my kids eventually start asking, "What are we doing today?"

"Ummm, laying on the beach!"

I spent most days of my childhood summers just going to the beach, and I would wonder, *What do people who live in, say, Chicago or Texas do all summer?* I would think, *Those are probably the bored kids who do drugs and steal.* Which is why I take my little Texans to the beach every summer. But try as I might to make them beach bums, they still want to know every hour on the hour, "What are we doing today?" So it ends up being more work than I bargained for.

Holidays and vacations are hard for some kids. You can, like clockwork, expect them to get very anxious and irritable when there is an element of change, excitement, or even anticipation. The stress for Adam began when we started to pack. He needed to know all the information about travel plans and schedules. He's always been that way. There is something in the strong-willed child that can't just go with the flow and take "Because I said so!" for an answer. It's one of the reasons we knew traveling might be hard for us, and we held out for so long.

Once we got there, none of us slept well or ate normally. Things were different and unpredictable. There are days on vacation, much like at home, when I could see in his eyes that it was going to be a tough day. In general, I have learned to stay on top of things that I know trigger my children. But as I would try to settle in and unpack and visit with family, I would default to allowing more iPad time. I'd gladly give them my phone to play on, not taking note of the time they spent on screens. Inevitably, they would drink caffeine and eat sugar because we're on vacation or at a restaurant. It's just what we do! And Grandpa would take them on a "special outing" that was outside of my control. It may have been okay for some children, but these were big triggers for Adam. And one day took a turn for the worse.

Look, *I* would have been fine with it all if *he* had been fine with it all. I gave up being a martyr a long time ago about things that don't matter like sugar or screen time or sleep schedules. But if you have a child like mine, who is already wound tight, you learn that structure is key. He has always been affected by certain things that I do need to monitor, but it was hard on vacation because *I* wanted to be on vacation. Why can't *I* be on vacation? I can—just not with my kids.

17

RUN FOR YOUR LIFE

The culmination of all these triggers was upon us this particular afternoon. My son was just so irritable and bouncing off the walls. I decided, with a beach house full of family visiting, to take my boys for a long walk on the beach. My husband and I walked for more than a mile with both boys running up ahead of us before we decided it was time to turn back. (I always forget that as far as we go is also as far as we have to come back. There's a life lesson here. I'm sure of it!)

Adam refused to head back and became very defiant, claiming we said it would be a *long* walk. When he would get like that, he would say things like, "You are a big, fat liar, and I hate you! You are the worst parents in the entire universe, and I wish you were never born!"

With an audience of very uncomfortable onlookers, we calmly kept walking, knowing he would eventually turn back around. The one thing I've always been pretty sure of is that my son could exhibit self-control in most of his outrageous outbursts. For instance, he would knock over a stack of papers but not a vase. He'd throw a flip-flop at me but never a cleat. I could see the Holy Spirit restraining him, and it gave me great hope. He eventually ran to catch up as we walked back to the house.

Back at the house, my husband told him to go upstairs to his room and stay there through dinner. He was "done!" This sounds like a great plan, but my son is never quite "done." At home, he would usually come down five times to tell us how "not done" he was, and that we are horrible parents! (All the while I am trying to serve dinner or help with homework or, as in this case, entertain my in-laws and relax.) He may have come down a time or two while I was preparing dinner. I don't remember. But he was upstairs in some strange, musty room with creaky bunk beds and hard mattresses with a few toys we brought from home and some lame coloring books. It was quiet while the rest of us ate dinner, and I thought perhaps he fell asleep or was in a spot spying on us (because that's a thing with him!) After dinner, while the tide came up in the backyard, the other children went out front to play volleyball, and ride skateboards up and down the private drive that sat between our house and the train tracks, separated only by an ivy-lined lattice fence.

This was the beach of my childhood where I never thought twice about the train tracks. The sound of the train passing every thirty minutes was soothing to me. As a teenager, it was my gauge of time as I could lose myself basking in the sun and listening to the sound of the crashing ocean. Crossing the tracks to get to my car or the bathroom at the 7-11 multiple times a day in my bare feet was the norm. By the end of each summer, my feet were callously tough and kind of black from the lava rocks that lined the train tracks.

That night, I listened to my children play on the drive while I cleaned up from dinner and visited with family. The sounds of children playing in the front and waves crashing in the back were music to my ears. Even the train going by once was a familiar sound that calmed my previously anxious heart.

Just then my daughter came through the front door and said, "Mom, I just saw Adam on the train tracks!" It sounded so preposterous. There was no way to get up there except to climb the tall ivy fence and brave the lava gravel. But sure enough, as I ran out the front door, I saw a little blue shirt and some blond hair pop up behind the shrubs that lined the train tracks.

I sprinted across the private drive, vaulted a trash dumpster, climbed the ivy fence, and braved the lava rocks in my bare feet. Even at that moment, the irony of my odd childhood preparation was not lost on me. I thought to myself, *Devil, please! I was born for a time such as this!*

Eight-year-old Adam saw me and began to run. I chased after him. I began to think of my friend Suzanne and how when times would get tough, she would say, "Honey, this ain't no hill for a stepper!" This was a hill like I had never quite seen before.

I knew the train had just come, so I had at least thirty minutes before it would come again. I ran on the lava rocks for two miles, chasing my son but never bridging the gap between us. I prayed and yelled and ran. He mostly ran on the slats of the tracks, and I ran on the lava shoulder, hoping to swoop in and clip him from the side. But I could never get close enough. People passed by either jogging or biking, and I would yell to them, "Please stop him! He is running away!" Still, they couldn't hear me over the ocean and the highway, and it was too late once they passed me. For a moment, I stopped and cried, knowing I could not catch him. Then I just dug deep and kept running. What else could I do?

Finally, a very fit young jogger ran past Adam. As he headed toward me, I jumped in front of him, and said, "Sir, please help me. My son is running away, and I have been chasing him for two miles!" He turned around at lightning speed, ran back, and tackled my son on the lava rocks. He dragged him kicking and screaming to me and said, "Is this yer mum? You better obey her, mate!" (Not only was he fit, but he was cute and Aussie too.)

We were still parallel to the stretch of beach houses, just two miles south now. My new Aussie hero helped me hoist my son back over the ivy fence, and I followed. Adam wasn't done running, though. He ran from me down on the beach for a bit. My daughter and father-in-law headed him off at the pass and brought him back to the house to my husband.

Speaking of my husband, where had he been? *He* was the professional athlete, created by God and trained by the best to actually chase and tackle people. Even my wide sideline swooping plan was a bit reminiscent of things I'd seen my husband do. Why wasn't he the one chasing his son for two miles? Would he have given up? Could his smooth, northern Californian feet not have endured the lava rocks? Would the Aussie hero have helped a big, scary, tatted-up man twice his size? Maybe some things are just between a boy and his mom?

These questions were running through my head while I was running. And now, as I stood gasping for air back in the driveway, looking at my whole family (in-laws included), I heard the train go by in the background. "Well, now you know!" I said, still gasping for air, "Now you know what I go through."

My mother-in-law hugged me and said she was sorry. I wondered if now, perhaps, they saw why I was so strict about certain things. Would they believe me now when I said not to feed him too much sugar or not to give him caffeine? Would they understand why I was so strung out about the "schedules and the screens" and why I would rather put him to bed myself than let them try? I wondered if now my crazy, plate-spinning life made sense to anyone.

18

IT IS WHAT IT IS

My focus quickly turned back to Adam, who was upstairs with my husband. We weren't about to let him out of our sight again. We had him shower as we moved his mattress and bedding into our master bedroom, so we could sleep near him. I was torn between screaming at him and hugging him. He said he was mad at Dad and just wanted to be away from him and not be sent to his room. That was it.

He had run away from home before down the street a handful of times. Once he went a few blocks and hid in the bushes. It's a flight-or-fight thing. The stress level gets too intense for him, or he doesn't want to take his punishment. It's like he has an out-of-body experience and is escaping the emotions of the situation. Or perhaps he knows full well what he is doing, and the will is just that strong and wants what it wants.

I woke up feeling rather hungover from the previous night's events. I lingered with my coffee, watching the waves crash on the shore of my favorite stretch of beach, trying hard to calm my nerves. My father-in-law joined me. Trying to make small talk, he asked if I planned to work out that day. I looked up and said, "No, I went running last night." No one laughed. It was too soon.

It was the last day of our vacation, so we loaded the car and headed out to our favorite private beach as planned.

Adam was back to his normal self. It's a pattern I can track to this day: triggers are in effect; anxiety builds; he explodes; then he's fine. I thought to myself, *The strong will wins again!* He technically was not banished in his room. And he got all the attention he wanted.

This all felt bigger and stronger than I was. I wondered what the hell was wrong with this child, and why God would put me through this. I wondered if I was the only one who had ever pole-vaulted a trash dumpster and run four miles in her bare feet to save a child from getting hit by a train. Maybe there were other moms out there with similar stories, but where were they? I needed them at that moment.

When we got back to Texas, I made an appointment with a counselor we had been seeing. On the drive there, my emotions got the best of me, and I asked, "Adam, what was that all about? I mean, your behavior that day was very dangerous, and you could have died!" I continued, "Dad spent a lot of money, and you ruined the whole trip for everyone! It was supposed to be fun."

He responded by breaking down and crying and yelling, "It wasn't fun for me! It wasn't fun for me! It wasn't fun for me! Did you ever think about that?"

It was at that moment that I realized how much all the triggers affected him, and how seriously I needed to take them. It was also the moment that I realized this was bigger than he was too. He needed my help, and I needed to take the time to understand him better. He was just a little boy trying to handle these big emotions and the big world around him. We were a team, like it or not. He is who he is, like it or not, and I was willing to fight for him with everything I had.

The counselor suggested we seek a clinical diagnosis before she saw us again. I felt she must've seen something I didn't, so we proceeded to seek a "clinical diagnosis." We had diagnostic workups of motor, verbal, and blood tests, while we, along with Adam's teachers, filled out umpteen million forms. They tested for ADHD, autism, Asperger's, any spectrum disorder, bipolar, and even oppositional defiant disorder. It was a long, drawn-out process for all of us. And then, just as we suspected, everything was just fine! "What you have here, ma'am, is a highly intelligent, healthy, strong-willed boy! Congratulations!" Terrific, right? It's what I wanted to hear, right?

Absolutely! But something in me longed to put my finger on the problem and call it something, so I could get a book about it or a pill to give him, or at least have a plan of action. I wanted someone to tell me what it was, so I could blame his behavior on something. Something other than what seemed to be my sub-par parenting skills. But that's just it! No form of good parenting was going to parent the strong will *out* of my son. Sure, there are things that help and things that hurt, but as my husband says, "It is what it is." I used to hate that phrase. He says it often, so often that I bought him a plaque that has that phrase on it for his desk. But I've come to embrace it and gain strength from it.

Could I have done things differently at the beach? Absolutely! Could we have avoided this whole incident? Maybe.

Perhaps if I did everything right and avoided all triggers, was more attentive, fed him raw veggies and fresh fish and distilled water and all the right supplements, and didn't travel, it would be a strong maybe. There would be something else. There's always something.

My son is who he is, and I am going to parent him *as is* and not try to change him or wish he was different so that my life could be easier. God did not promise me easy. But he has promised to never leave me nor forsake me and be my ever-present help in times of trouble. In this I find my strength for another day.

19

HOLY CRAP

When my son was a toddler, he was notorious for not sleeping during nap time. He would either come out a million times or quietly make a mess. He also liked to take his diaper off and then poop and pee everywhere. Every day at nap time I would say, "No, no!" And he would repeat back to me, "No, no!" like he understood. But day after day there would be some sort of catastrophe.

One day, I went to get him from his "nap" and couldn't believe my eyes. Have you ever come upon your toddler's room and noticed that something was wrong, but you aren't sure what? There is a diaperless baby, or they've taken their shirt off or lowered the rails, or filled the crib with stuffed animals when you didn't even know they could get out, let alone climb back in with all their friends?

I stood at the door taking it all in as the unpleasant yet familiar smell wafted to my nostrils. There he stood, naked with diaper in hand, with what my husband would refer to as a "shit-eating grin" on his face and a trail of poop smeared everywhere. Just think "crime scene" but with poop on everything from the carpet to the crib rails to the dump truck and the doorknob. What's a mom to do? So many of my parenting moments go like that! Seriously, what am I supposed to do now, God?

It seemed to me that there should be one book handed out at the hospital, perhaps an owner's manual of sorts, that would help me parent my child from beginning to end. I was desperate for some concrete methods to grab hold of and confidently say, "I am doing this, and it is working." But what I have found over the years is that some advice has worked sometimes in some seasons, and then sometimes it didn't.

Often when I pick up a book, if I can tell that the author has not been through what I've been through or is talking about small stuff like it's a big deal, I'll put it down. I am easily discouraged and want to hear from someone who gets me. Then at other times, something I read resonates with me. I try it and feel empowered. There is no one way or best book because every child is different, and every parent-child relationship is different.

But I was desperate to find something other than spanking that would work to discipline my son. I was looking to be in control of my emotions while teaching my son that he needed to obey and control his actions. I wanted it to feel more like teamwork than authoritarianism.

I mentioned *Love and Logic Magic for Early Childhood*[7] as a book I connected with and implemented at times. I didn't have a hundred percent success rate, but I was kind of into it for a while. Here's why. It put the consequences back on the child and encouraged me to keep calm. The authors give some examples of how to show your toddler that there are consequences for their actions. If you do *this,* then you don't get *that.* I was ready to put this theory to the test.

The next day at nap time I said to my son, "We will have popsicles after naptime *if* you keep your diaper on!" The first day he did not listen to me, and there I was, charged with sticking to my guns. It was so hard for me to see him sad and disappointed sans popsicle. It honestly felt more painful (to me at least) than a spanking, but then I remembered how sad *I* felt cleaning up the poop crime scene. Lo and behold, the very next day at nap time I gave him the same warning. And, wouldn't you know, that boy kept his diaper on! When I opened his door after naptime, the first thing he said was "Popsicles?" with a big grin on his face. Sweet Victory!

"Yes, buddy, popsicles!"

I used very concrete, black and white, doable tasks with consequences. Did it work every time? No, but it did work sometimes. And I will take sometimes over never.

We laugh now and then about how the authors of the series encourage the readers to adopt a catchphrase for use when their child is arguing with them or throwing a fit. Again, this should be done while staying calm and keeping the emotions in check. This was key for me. Mine was, "It's a bummer you're choosing to act this way!" My husband says I sounded sarcastic every time I said it. I would also say "I love you too much to fight with you." To which my toddler would reply, "Well, I hate *you* too much!" to which I would reply. "Well, that's a bummer!" I use these phrases to this day. It infuriates my teen boys who look at me and say, "What does that even mean?" It means I am passive-aggressively stopping this conversation in its tracks before it derails! It's pretty effective and keeps me calm!

One particular day when my son was about six or seven, his behavior was extremely unbecoming. We had planned a family swim evening. I told him he could not participate and had to remain in his room. Incidentally, any of our other children would have simply remained in their room and been sad, taking their consequences—not this guy! As we jumped and splashed and threw the other children in the air, I looked towards the back of the house and saw that he had indeed come out of his room. His little body was now pressed up against the kitchen window facing the pool with big tears streaming down his face.

I, of course, caved in and let him swim with us that day. One thing I know he cannot endure is being excluded from what the family is doing. It is his "currency," so to speak, and knowing this made it so hard to discipline him in this way because my ultimate goal is family reconciliation, not rejection or isolation. But sometimes it has to be done, and you as the parent will have to gauge the "when to" and the "when not to" of sticking to your guns. My husband or I have stayed home with a child, opting out of "family plans" as their punishment to show that actions have consequences, and sometimes everybody suffers.

Sometimes we do it so the rest of the family can have the fun they deserve or have earned as a reward. We've made one child go to bed while everyone else watches a movie (only to catch a kid peeking from the upstairs railing). We do the dance, and we try our best.

My kids have learned over the years, however, that repentance and forgiveness allow them quick re-entry into the family plans. In Tedd Tripp's book *Shepherding a Child's Heart* he speaks to this as well. Sin, disobedience, and rebellion put us out of fellowship with God and one another. Our desire as parents is to not only modify behavior but, more importantly, reconnect broken fellowship.[7] This rings true in my heart, and I struggle to let my baby stand inside crying while I frolic or eat popsicles outside. So we wrestle with what is right and what works best and how to be firm but not legalistic.

My son has also learned that when he apologizes and has a change of behavior, he is allowed more freedom and has richer relationships too. It came with time, consistency, and age. Now at fifteen (and still strong-willed, by the way), he will go away angry and come back within twenty minutes or so with a heartfelt apology and take responsibility for his actions. My husband says he might be playing me because he wants something. (But, hey, I welcome it and call it a win-win situation.) I'll take a heartfelt, remorseful apology any day over the days of tantrums and yelling and screaming. They will learn from you that these moments of meltdowns are not tolerated in your family and that you have a higher standard.

A certain type of behavior and attitude is welcomed, celebrated, encouraged, and rewarded, and another simply is not. Consistently displaying this in your home will become a pattern that they will hopefully understand and adopt. There is a standard, a consequence, and a reward. There can be restoration and unity! There doesn't have to be anger, chaos, and tumult. I may not have been the most consistent in the area of discipline, but I think I was consistent in showing my son that disobedience leads to a breach in our relationships and affects us all. And I directed him to a much healthier alternative.

20

FROM PLAYPENS TO PLAYGROUNDS

When my daughter Rebekah was an infant, I felt a bit overwhelmed as to how to vacuum with a baby in tow. Isn't that funny? I didn't think I should do it while she was sleeping, and she was *always* sleeping. I guess I could've held her, but I just couldn't wrap my mind around what to do. I was new at this, and Chad was gone playing football *a lot*. I didn't dare ask my peers about such a dumb problem. Surely, no one wanted to hear my sob story about my sleepy baby and my pro-athlete husband and how I just can't seem to find the time to vacuum my big house. I like to call them my champagne problems, but I was legitimately perplexed.

The same trusted friend who assured me I would survive childbirth suggested I train Rebekah to play alone in the playpen and then vacuum once she got the hang of that. The plan entailed setting the playpen up in another room and then leaving so she couldn't see me. The intent was to teach her that she could indeed play alone and be fine. That felt so torturous to me, but I was desperate for some alone time to do noisy chores. I put her down and left the room. But just to make sure she was okay, I army-crawled back in to spy on her. The minute I poked my head up, so did she. Our eyes locked, and she began to cry. Shoot!

I ran and vacuumed quickly while she wailed, and then I ran right back to pick her up. That was horrible! She was so pitiful that I ended up only doing it the one time. The playpen time was not for us. But, hey, I tried! We laugh about it to this day because Rebekah still rarely likes to be left alone.

I did come up with an idea, all on my own, to suction her bath chair to the (very low) coffee table, put her in there, and make funny faces at her while I vacuumed. Aye yai yai! The things we do! I'm not sure it was the safest thing to do, but it worked. And I was proud of myself. Ultimately, I had to find what worked for me *and* Rebekah. We eventually found our groove.

Do all the things to find what works for you and your people. It takes some time to find your groove, and it won't look like everyone else's groove. But it will be yours. There is strength to be gained in persevering, putting your head down and your sweat equity in, and finding a rhythm for your family.

It's not just you and what you want anymore. I wish it were that easy to add children to your life and have nothing change. Years ago I was at a get-together with some families from church. It was getting late when my girlfriend's son started acting up and throwing a tantrum right there on the kitchen floor. She turned to a pastor who had been fielding all our parenting questions, pointed, and said, "See? What am I supposed to do here?"

To which he responded, "Take him home. It's late. I don't think he wants to be here." Brilliant! We make things so hard sometimes, don't we?

We used to go to a friend's house who had little boys as well, hoping they would all play, and the adults would have dinner and socialize. We would be five minutes in, and my son would do something horrible like hit or bite or start a fight over a toy. He'd ruin our time or, at best, make it awkward. I would often recall that pastor's wise advice and take my son home or at times even decline the invitation. Sure, it was disappointing and frustrating but not as much as my futile attempts to make the evening work.

That was not my favorite season of parenting, but it didn't last forever. We go out now and even entertain, and it's wonderful. Remember, we talked about this earlier, about how it's not really about you? I mean you can *try* to fit them into your old rhythms and routines, but in my experience, it behooves you to try and find a new family groove.

My son grew out of a lot of his frustrations and tantrums, but what helped along the way was me being sensitive to what stressed him out. I realized how tightly wound he was and factored in what had gone on in his day at school or with his siblings. Like the incident at the beach where he kept saying, "It wasn't fun for me!" I'll never forget that. Sometimes your child just doesn't want to go to a friend's house, and that's okay! Find what they *do* like, and what does work. Notice why, and you will all be better off.

I took a picture of my son running on the beach one summer when he was very little. I noticed him running toward the water and then away from the tide while it chased his feet over and over again. Then he'd switch it up and run parallel to the shore. I captioned it "We finally found a playground big enough for Adam!" It was true then and still to this day; he can play in the water for hours. The wide-open space is as big as his will.

Maybe the beach calms him the same way it calms me. There's something peaceful about seeing the ocean and the skyline and knowing that, although God is so big and powerful, we are safe in his arms. My son seems free and unrestrained. I could breathe freely watching *him* run free. Until, of course, he got sand on his sandwich or in the liner of his shorts or decided he was done. But I'll take it even if it is short-lived. The same was true for big parks and snowy mountains, anywhere he could run and be free.

Running *free* was one thing. But once we asked him to suit up in a uniform and be on a team to run, it was a different story. We thought for a moment (because of the running) that he might enjoy soccer, but were we ever wrong. Adam would throw a fit over going to practices and games. A few times a season he would miss both, whether he just flat out refused to go or was grounded for his bad attitude. Once during a time out in a game, he came and sat on my lap and then never wanted to go back in, so we just sat there and watched the rest of his team play the game.

What's a girl to do? Should I force him back in? When do I call his bluff, and when do I give him grace? These are tough parenting calls to make. This is when you listen to the Holy Spirit and go with your gut. It's not about you or your pride or your image. It's about finding that sweet spot and those activities that make their hearts sing and bring them pleasure. Find that for your kiddo. It's so awesome when you find it for a strong-willed child.

If they don't like something, they don't like something! This is especially true for the strong-willed child. If you haven't figured it out yet, they will let you know. It's futile to continue making them do something they don't like. It's insane actually. I've heard it said that the definition of insanity is doing the same thing over and over again expecting different results. Don't be insane! Parenting is all about finding that sweet spot for them. If they don't like soccer, maybe you don't make them play soccer at five years old. Hindsight is supreme here. I look back now and think, *Who even cared?* No one but me! My frustration was in trying to find something to make him happy. (I'd think, *Ugh! Back to the drawing board.*)

If no one has ever told you that you don't need to over-schedule your kids, and they don't need to play soccer or dance or go on playdates if they don't want to, allow me. You can stop and just stay home, and let them play with a ball or playdough or a rock and a stick. My son loved a Rubik's cube too. He would solve it over and over and over again. (And Legos! Lots and lots of Legos!)

Adam did like football for a short while. But, honestly, it was a bit chaotic for him. He eventually found his groove in basketball. It was solitary, methodical, competitive, and fun, just like him. *And* he can do it all by himself! *And* I don't ever have to nag him—*ever*. Well, sometimes I have to nag him to come inside and eat or not to play super early in the morning and wake up the neighbors, but that's it!

Now every morning at 7:30 a.m., I take my son to the high school for varsity basketball practice, and it is my absolute pleasure to do so. My neighbors also thank me! One particular morning, we arrived at school a bit early. As we sat waiting in the car, I spotted a man with two large, yellow Labrador retrievers out on the grassy football practice field. The dogs were big and athletic, but the man was not particularly so. I watched as he threw a toy long and far for them to bring back. They must have gone back and forth at least ten times at full speed. I thought to myself that that's probably not what the man wants to be doing at 7:30 in the morning or even his idea of fun, but it is what the dogs needed and therefore was in his best interest. Maybe he worked from home, and there was no other way to keep them calm. Maybe he was going to be gone all day, and this was their one time to go out. Or maybe, just maybe, he knew they liked it, and therefore he liked it too. Either way, I thought to myself, *What a smart man.*

I wonder if he knew to do that right away or stumbled upon it by accident: "Wow, they really run far and fast." I wonder how long it took him to find the right toy to throw and the right field to use. Did he struggle with his pups until someone suggested running them hard and early? What else had he tried? I bet the harder it was to find his rhythm, the more joy he derived from watching them run.

The harder it is to find *your* rhythm, the more joy you will derive from watching *them* run. Keep at it, Mama! You will find your groove and theirs too. I didn't know what to do with my sleepy little infant or how to vacuum. I watched other people's children play soccer while mine sat suited up in my lap on the sidelines. You will get there if you do not grow weary. Do not throw in the towel, and do not give up the fight!

My daughter is a grown woman now with a career and an apartment and even a vacuum of her own. We facetime daily, and she doesn't wail anymore, but I do sometimes because I miss her so much. And twice a week I don my cheesy "Basketball Mom" t-shirt and brave the bleachers to cheer on Adam and his team as they run up the court and back a hundred times at full speed, fearlessly facing their opponents. It amazes me how with sweat in his eyes and a smile on his face he can pivot so effortlessly to run backward (who runs backward?) down the court, stop on a dime, and block his opponent with his 6-foot-3-inch, 200-pound, grown-man body. When did that happen by the way? (It appears to have happened overnight. But you and I both know that's not true.) All this growth, all this confidence, excellence, pride, and joy, developed over time, while we were helping them find their groove.

Eric Liddell:

"I believe God made me for a purpose, but he also made me fast. And when I run, I feel His pleasure."
— Chariots of Fire

21

WHAT WOULD GRANDMA DO?

The first year Adam attended preschool, I was still home-schooling the girls. He only went half-day, and we welcomed the reprieve. I had our schedules perfectly planned out (or so I thought). Adam did so well in school, all the teachers adored him, and he never had any behavior problems to speak of, but *after* school was a different story. I would pick him up with a grand plan to give him a nap and continue the rest of the school day with the girls.

Try as I might, I could not get him to nap—or stay in his room or sit down to watch a show or entertain himself. Didn't he know we had work to do? Apparently, *no one told him!* He would see everyone at home and want to be in the mix, get all wound up, and then become explosive and mad—every—single—day. He would fight me over a snack or a nap or an after-school activity. He was a little tyrant in a pull-up, running around the house ruling the roost. And I couldn't get anything done!

If I had to take the girls somewhere, he would scream bloody murder and kick the back of my headrest until I couldn't drive. I even had a car with a third row, and I would buckle him in his car seat way back there, but then he would torment his sisters. I've heard (as I'm sure you have) that some kids focus so hard on being good at school, they let it all out on you when they get home because you are safe. I do find this to be true but not particularly helpful at the moment.

I was set on being a good homeschool mom at all costs. I began looking for an after-school daycare for the boys. It seems crazy to me now, but that's how passionate I felt about homeschool at the time. Perhaps I gained so much of my identity from it that I couldn't imagine not homeschooling. But if I'm to be honest, I was burning out! I remember my little schoolroom always smelled like a dirty diaper. I was constantly taking breaks to feed a baby or put out a fire, and I felt like I was shortchanging the girls. I remember sitting on the stairs, crying on the phone to my mom one night after putting everyone to bed and telling her my new plan.

I always seemed to have a new plan. I told her I was tired and didn't feel like anyone was getting the best of me, and nothing felt excellent. She proposed that I give the boys the same quality time I gave the girls in those early formative years, and let the girls go to school now. She assured me that I had laid a good foundation for them and it was time to let them spread their wings. So, at my mom's advice, I put my girls in school full-time, which allowed me to focus on my little preschoolers. It truly brought some peace and a slower pace to my household. Something my mom could see I needed.

Off the girls went, leaving me more time with the boys when they arrived home from their half-day preschool. It was the sweetest little preschool in town, by the way. First Foundations in Austin, Texas was where lives were magically transformed in the dreamy classroom of Miss Mauer's Muppets. I only wish I had more children to send there. It was that good! When they would come back home, I had more time and energy to focus on them.

If no one has ever given you permission to change your plan, allow me! You can be a good mom and homeschool, and you can be a good mom and send your kids to private school. You can even be a good mom and send your kids to public school! I am living proof.

One spring when my mom was visiting, the girls were at school, and David was sleeping. Adam had just returned home from preschool, and I had some big building blocks out for him to play with while I visited with my mom. I always had a large cabinet full of toys downstairs. I could just open it for instant entertainment. It came in handy when the girls were getting ready for school, or I was making dinner or, as in this case, visiting with my mom. We had a large playroom upstairs, but no one ever liked to go up there alone. (Can you blame them?) This particular day, Adam was building a super tall tower, and I sat on the floor with him. It sounds so simple (to sit with him). But looking back now, I know it was a game-changer.

There is a difference between me being busy cooking dinner while I talk with him versus face-to-face at the table or watching a show side-by-side, engaging with him, instead of being on my computer while I talk with him. He still enjoys undistracted attention. (Who doesn't?) Just the other day he got mad because I had been on my phone during his basketball game. (In my defense, he was sitting out at the moment, and I was texting the score to his dad.) Most distractions we tolerate as moms can be justified as good and important. Be mindful of that.

Social media was not as prevalent when my kids were little. They were all well past middle school before all the apps were on all the phones. I can only imagine the distractions I would be battling trying to be present for my little ones these days. My girls and I can sit and watch a movie and be on our phones and laptops at the same time, and it doesn't bother any of us. Every child is different. You need to be sensitive to each of them. Realizing my son's need for one-on-one time in a calm, peaceful environment was key to successful parenting for us. Could we always make that happen for him? No, but I was aware of the importance and tried to make it possible as often as I could.

My mom sat on the couch, flipping through a stack of magazines as I sat on the floor at her feet building a tall tower with my son. Every time it fell, he would throw a tantrum, screaming and shaking until his face was purple. (He used to do this so much that the blood vessels in his face would pop from the strain!) My normal response would be to get frustrated and mad. I would pop up and take him to his room, letting him know that that type of behavior was not to be tolerated. And then the whole song and dance would begin. I dreaded the cycle. I looked at my mom when the tall tower tumbled as if to say, "See? This is my life every day! A tall tumbling tower!" She had long heard what I had been going through, but today she witnessed it firsthand.

Stepping in as only a grandma could, she got down on the ground with him. Instead of losing her cool, she said, "It's ok, Adam. Let's build it together." And she showed him how he could build it right back up. When it fell over again, she laughed and said, "Uh, oh!" shrugged and began to rebuild. He watched her with a leery scowl on his face for a bit, and to be honest with you, I thought, *This could go many directions.* We were ready to have blocks thrown at our heads for sure, but we have to keep trying, don't we? We can't give up on our difficult children. That's just not an option. To our surprise, he began to calm down and joined in. "Uh, oh!" he would mimic, with a little preschool shrug. My mom and I looked at each other with great satisfaction. She knew that for us this was a huge breakthrough.

Friend, it's exhausting. (I know!) My frustration was not so much with his behavior, but I was trying to visit with my mom, and everything always seemed so hard and challenging. I also hated seeing him like this.

We say, "Just be happy!" We think, *Why can't you just act normal?*

But I took a deep, slow breath because something about that day gave me hope that perhaps we were onto something.

Yes, my son was, and still is, easily frustrated. Smart, stubborn people usually are. But when rigid frustration meets rigid frustration, it's a recipe for disaster. Somebody needs to flex, and, my dear friend, it is going to be you. What my mom modeled for me, and what I began to model for him from that point on was peacefulness, patience, and flexibility.

I was thankful that my mom encouraged me to spend this precious time with my little ones. In those moments I saw glimpses of who they are and what makes them tick. I wouldn't trade it for the world. I took the time to discover what brings out the best in them, what makes them feel better when they are upset, and even what triggers them. There are a myriad of factors, including sleep, food, stress, and perhaps emotions carried over from the school day.

I learned to be more preventative than reactive. Why set them up for failure? If you know they don't like to rush or have plans changed on them abruptly, maybe you try not to do that. Give them extra time to complete tasks when you can, and give them a long runway with kind reminders. Prepare them when something stressful is going to happen. It's okay to defuse conflicts and even avoid them when possible. There is enough conflict that will find you on its own. Look for moments of breakthrough and victory instead. My son liked to know how many minutes away things were and exactly what we will be doing when we get there. He is still like this at fifteen. I have learned to tell him. It's that simple, and it's fine.

I was thankful for my mom's wisdom and guidance that led to so many breakthroughs within my family. I'm not a grandma just yet, but sometimes it doesn't hurt to try thinking like one.

22

RAISING RED HOT CHILI PEPPERS

In my kitchen sits a tall decorative jar of red-hot chili peppers. It has been sitting there for years, but every so often I pause to look at it, smile, and think, *Yep, that's us!* Our house is full of red-hot chili peppers! We are fiery, bold, strong, and spicy. We must hold the records for the gamut of emotions that can erupt in one household on a given day and for topping the decibel scale when everyone insists on being heard all at once. It has overwhelmed me at times, but as my husband says, "It is what it is." I've become accustomed to it. Maybe the right word is comfortable or even numb. Perhaps it was a curse spoken by my dad when he uttered the phrase "Just you wait!" Maybe—just maybe—God knew what he was doing when he put these six of us together, and things are just as they should be.

Someone was always pushing the limits and my buttons. Something was always dirty or broken. Even though someone was always yelling or crying, hurt or offended, one thing is for sure, above all the chaos there was always love. Some days I felt outnumbered and exhausted. But just when the pressure would get to me, a sweet child would say, "Mom, you are my best friend!" Or a teen would text me from school to say they miss me and remind me of a funny inside joke. (Which is my all-time favorite thing!)

Or a sweet bundle of little boy arms and legs would climb into bed to snuggle at 5 a.m., and my heart would melt. It would all be worth it. With all of our fire and spice, there are caring hearts and lots of loyalty. Spicy is not bad! Strong-willed is not bad.

I did struggle at times to find productive ways to discipline my little peppers so that the wheels would not come off this love bus. I have screamed and spanked, banished and boycotted. I have even gone on strike and pulled the car over. Such tactics produced momentary regret (for both parent and child) but did not change the family dynamic or the God-given bent of my children any more than it changed the color of their eyes or hair. There were those moments when I just wanted everyone to *sit still and be quiet!* But compliant (sit-still-"yes ma'am") children were not in the cards for me, nor is that what this book is about.

Just this morning there was a meltdown involving missing advent candy. Tears were shed, and blows were thrown between brothers. Seriously? On the way out the door? The school is two minutes away, people! I was mad, and it was bad. When I picked the boys up from school, they spent the afternoon trying to make it right. They asked about my day, did chores, used their manners, gave hugs and kisses, and had cheery dispositions. They even did all their homework! (It was weird.) I told them I loved them and that I forgave them and had moved on (anything to make this odd behavior stop).

There are certainly clear boundaries in our home. When they cross the line, we let them know. We withhold privileges and "life as they know it," and sometimes we heap on the chores and responsibility until the lesson is learned. Then we forgive. And we talk a lot about what went wrong and how it could have been handled differently. Then we move forward because this is a training ground (a messy training ground), not an assembly line that spits out perfect children.

I have come to find, through much trial and error, a few things that did produce fruit and bring about lasting change while parenting a strong-willed child. These things are best modeled. We are their teachers—their examples.

Model and teach forgiveness. Don't ever hold a grudge against your kiddos. Even if you feel justified. The Bible tells us that we are to bear with one another and forgive as the Father forgives us. We're to walk in love and unity. Let peace reign supreme in our hearts no matter what. God forgives us instantly. We should follow suit and extend forgiveness quickly as well. I mean, how long are we supposed to harbor resentment and offenses? The Bible also says love "overlooks an offense." We are all a work in progress.[8]

Do your children see you apologize to your spouse? Do you make amends and move on? Likewise, do you apologize to *them* when you are wrong or harsh? Do you ask them to forgive you? It's healthy for them to see this on display at home. It builds a safe environment for them. It teaches them that, although we make mistakes, we are all still loved and valued. It sets an example for their future relationships as well as their relationship with Christ.

Model and teach love. You can show your children love by serving them and having kind words on your tongue. Invest in them by truly listening to them, so they know they are treasured and valued. Show them how to treat each other. I love to hear my daughter saying to her brother, "How can I help you with that, bud?" I know she has heard me ask him that a million times and in doing so has learned to be kind and loving. The Bible says in 1 Peter 4:8, "Above all, love each other deeply, because love covers over a multitude of sins." We are all going to make mistakes and fall short. Love anyway. Love often. Love hard.

Model and teach strong character. Let them see you doing the right thing. Talk about your decision-making so they can see what that process looks like. Show them that it's not always easy, but your desire to follow and honor God is what's most important. Stop gossip or mean-spirited talk in its tracks, and make sure you don't engage in it either. When *you* act righteously and kindly, when *you* are quick to listen, slow to speak, and slow to become angry, they are watching. And they are learning. This may seem like a tall order for us and definitely for them, but let's show them that strong character is attainable by following the example of Christ. Sometimes when I set out to model or teach something, I realize how much I needed the lesson as well.

Model and teach humility. We are told in the Bible to imitate Christ's humility and value others above ourselves. The world can be harsh, and our children will inevitably encounter people who are selfish and prideful and mean-spirited. We should be a soft place for our children to land at the end of a long, hard day. When attitudes flair and tempers are short (including yours) take a deep breath, count to ten, pray that long, wordy prayer for help if you need to, and then be what your family needs. Even Jesus took the lowly form of a baby when he could have thrown his weight around and demanded respect and obedience. Instead, he laid down His life for us when we least deserved it. He is our ultimate example of kindness and humility.

Ask yourself how you can lay down your life for your children. What can you do to show them how much they matter to you? Make them feel valued and important. In my house, it's the little things like making the food they like ("just because"). Chicken broccoli casserole (as boring as it sounds) or sloppy joes or homemade granola bars put smiles on the faces of my often-weary people. I've also been known to do chores and laundry for busy students during finals. (No questions asked as I overlook the less than enthusiastic looks on their faces, surely brought on by their study stressors—surely.)

It's hardly laying down my life, but it makes them feel special and noticed, and that is a win for me. Humility is also admitting when you are wrong and apologizing to your children. It's hard, especially when they are little. But if you start this whole process when they are little, it will be easier when they are teens. (Pro tip: M&M's and breakfast tacos help break the ice when apologizing to teens.) Serving them and extending forgiveness helps soften rough edges (and keeps *your heart* from becoming bitter) and sets the stage for future relationship success.

Study your kiddos. Study your kiddos so you can parent accordingly. Find out what makes them tick, upset, and feel loved. One child might struggle where another one doesn't. Someone will inevitably need more of your attention at times. Stop and take notice of that. Be present! Make it your job to know them. Make knowing them intimately your life's work.

Strong-willed children need strong leadership more than harsh or strict control. Their strong will will eventually serve them well in the real world. Take the time to teach and model "the important stuff." If you will pour yourself out like a drink offering (full of love, grace, and understanding), it will trump the chaos and noise and yield a harvest of kindness and character.

My home was, and still is, dripping with drive, destiny, potential, and passion. I want to make the most of each personality. What will they become, these chili peppers of mine? There are just two left in my house, and the years are going fast. There is still modeling, teaching, noise, and love going on in here. I am misty-eyed when I count the milestones left with my two teens. My prayer is that I can continue to see them through God's eyes and appreciate the way he made them. I pray the same for you and your family too.

PART 5

WE ARE STRONGER TOGETHER

When Moses' hands grew tired, they took a stone and put it under him and he sat on it. Aaron and Hur held his hands up—one on one side, one on the other—so that his hands remained steady till sunset.

Exodus 17:12

23

FIND YOUR TRIBE

*Tribe—a group of people with a common bond
either cultural, religious or generational, living in
community, providing for each other with intense
loyalty and faithfulness as one's own family*

Twenty-some-odd years ago, when Chad and I decided to get married, we called our very best friends and said, "Will you believe in us, rejoice with us, and stand with us?" They even agreed to stand in the unusually warm California heat that Sunday afternoon in June. My friends wore long, pink dresses, the color of Pepto Bismol, and the men donned black tuxes because they were our tribe. It was a no-brainer for them. We'd already been through a lot of life together: graduating high school, surviving college, dreaming big dreams, suffering big setbacks, and cheering each other on along the way. Most of my girlfriends had spent endless nights through the years encouraging me that God had a plan for my life, and this life included a fantastic husband. Thank God they were right about that one! They rarely steer me wrong, and I couldn't have made it through those early years without the support of my faithful tribe.

Distance and life have changed my friend groups a bit over the years. But in a culture that is becoming more autonomous and polarized, celebrating independence and solitude, I still desperately need community. We all need community. We need not just any community but a community with a "common bond and intense loyalty" that will walk through this hard journey with us—arm-in-arm—a tribe! I believe it's how we are hard-wired. It's the way we were created (in God's image for a relationship with him and with others). He said it Himself in the beginning: "It is not good for the man to be alone!" (Gen. 2:18)

I find it interesting that in the book of Genesis, God brought all the animals to Adam for him to name and find a suitable companion. When no suitable companion was found, God created Woman. Two things stick out to me in this passage:

1. We are created specifically for *human* companionship. I know it's been said that "dog is man's best friend," but I beg to differ! We need human relationships.

2. It takes time to find the right people.

God put Adam and Eve in relationships and, in time, tribes. He deliberately knits people together because he knows we need each other. I like to call it "Jesus with skin on." The Bible often mentions how important community is to God: "God sets the lonely in families." (Ps. 68:6) "How good and pleasant it is when God's people live together in unity! ... For there the Lord bestows his blessing, even life forevermore." (Ps. 133:1, 3b)

It's life-giving when you find people who believe in you when you're struggling to believe in yourself. Great friends will run to you when you have fallen. They will get what you're going through because they've been there too. They lift you up when you are weary and offer just the right words at just the right time and point you to Jesus when you've lost your way. How comforting it is to laugh, cry, worship, rejoice, grieve, and pray together. How good it feels to stand in the gap and lay down our lives for each other. It's God's plan!

A while back when Chad and I went on a vacation to Cancun, it took a small army of about five fabulous friends who understood my family dynamic to keep things running on the home front with no questions asked. They knew how rare it was for me to take time away from my kids. I was so thankful for their faithful, non-judgmental help. I also knew they had spared me a lot of details when they smiled and said, "Everything went fine!" (Liars!)

Recently, when I was terribly sick, my friend Jodi came running to the rescue with all her homeopathic remedies and encouraged me by telling me that I surely would not die. (I thought I might. And we all know that moms aren't allowed to get sick, let alone die!) My dear friend Chris brought me comfort food (a large Cherry Limeade from Sonic). Lo and behold, I made it through, greatly due to these women. It reminds me of the Scripture out of the Book of Acts that says, "Times of refreshing may come from the presence of the Lord!" (Acts 3:19-21) Maybe he just might use your tribe!

Sometimes, though, we lay aside all this goodness and try to do everything by ourselves. We think it's noble to say, "No thank you. I'm fine!" Striving to be some sort of martyr or "uber mom," we run carpools, committees, or marathons. We celebrate the strong, the independent, the driven. We make chore lists, goal charts, and resolutions. And when we fall short, we are left feeling tired and defeated, finding ourselves alone, looking around with mixed emotions to see if anyone saw us fall. We are grateful in one sense and disappointed in another.

Where are my friends?

Where is my community?

Where is my tribe?

Years ago, when my husband was first starting in the mortgage industry, he called up an older, well-established colleague for a favor. His colleague's response has haunted me and served as a sort of sobering reminder all these years. He said, "Chad, it's best to make your friends long before you need them." Wow! What a reminder to stop the hamster wheel of busyness and give attention to those relationships God has placed in our lives.

I tend to march to the beat of my own drum (code words for overcommitted and too busy), and I often find myself alone in the grind just trying to survive. Inevitably something in me longs for others, like deep calling to deep or a resonating tuning fork that must be responded to. (Hello... Hello...Is anybody out there?) If we take time to look up, we will see that God has put others near us who hear the cry of our hearts. It's as if they're saying, "Yes, yes, I'm here too, going through the same thing you're going through."

Those are your people! Grab hold of them and don't let go. You need each other.

If the plan was autonomy, there would be no need for marriages and families, counselors, pastors, tutors, teachers, trainers, or even motivational speakers, small groups, or churches. I could go on and on. God put us in relationships to help, encourage, and support one another as we follow him together. We're to carry one another's burdens, rejoice in each other's victories, and comfort one another during times of discouragement and trial. It's vulnerable and scary to let others see your flaws and shortcomings. But there's so much to be gained! There's nothing like surviving the grind *together* to forge a friendship and realize you have become a tribe. It's worth a hearty high-five! Parenting is hard. Marriage is hard. Adulting is hard. But it's easier together. We are stronger together.

24

A PEARL OF GREAT PRICE

Surrounding yourself with the *right* people during this season of your life is crucial to the health of your soul. Conversely, allowing the *wrong* people in your life can be detrimental. As well-intending as people might be, the wrong relationships can be draining. It can bring condemnation and shame, and who has time for that? If no one has ever given you permission to move on from negative friends or toxic relationships, allow me. Move on! The right people are out there looking for you too, and they will be like a cold drink of water to your parched and weary soul.

Some people just don't get what you are going through and probably never will. I didn't get it before I had my boys. I thought I was the best girl mom around town and that parenting was easy. If anyone was struggling, I thought it was solely a parenting issue and would offer lots of unsolicited advice. (Gross, I know!)

I remember visiting an old friend after I had Rebekah, and he asked me how parenting was going.

I said, "It's super easy! But she's a super easy baby."

And he said, "Give yourself more credit. Maybe you are just a really good mom."

I thought maybe he was right, and it stroked my ego a bit. I stood a little taller with my nose a little higher in the air. But now I look back and laugh, "Nah, she was just a really easy baby!"

I was immensely annoying, prideful, and self-righteous. I apologize to anyone and everyone I ever met before my world was rocked by a strong-willed child! My pride came tumbling down as I realized the parenting tools that worked on one child, or even two, were suddenly not working on this little guy. I found myself angry, frustrated, and in need of help. Not just from anyone, though, I needed the right people. It's like being stuck on a black diamond ski slope you have no business being on. Where are my experts at?

Sometimes even your closest friends won't understand, and that will frustrate you. You'll feel like they, of all people, should understand! It's okay. Maybe they aren't black diamond skiers. It's not their fault. Perhaps they are experts in some other field, just not this one.

I have a dear friend with very compliant little girls. She always politely asks, "How's Adam?" We've shared marriage struggles and teenage girl issues, and "done life" together for years and enjoy each other's company, but to *this,* I'd say, "He's good!" And she'd reply, "That's good!" Then we just move on. But I've had to *learn* to do that, learn to appreciate her for what we have in common and everything else she brings to the table. I've had to learn not to feel disappointed or frustrated that she didn't get what I was going through.

My friend Crystal got it. We met when our girls were taking dance classes together at our church, and I had to wrangle my boys into one of the Sunday school class-rooms while we waited. One day she looked at me and said, "Wow, you really struggle with them, don't you?"

I think my response was a long blank stare and a hearty, "Ya think?"

She said, "Tami, I know! I go through the same thing with one of my girls!"

We talked for a while that day and have been close friends ever since. I can tell her absolutely anything and never feel judged or ashamed. She gives profound, humble, carefully considered advice, points me to Jesus, and supports me in prayer.

There were seasons when my emotions were too raw to talk to anyone who didn't understand my plight. I was too fragile, broken, and exhausted to give them any space. It was easier once I found my go-to relationships to surround myself with like a spiritual swaddle. Now I can appreciate both. But there was a time when I could not.

One day on the phone with Crystal, I said, "I'm going to have to go because my son has pushed all the patio furniture in the pool *again* and is running down the street flipping me off!"

She replied, "Girl! Go get him, and call me back. I'm going to pray."

And she meant it!

When I called her back, she said, "I'm so glad things have calmed down. I was thinking about the time my daughter ran away like that, and I had to call the cops on her. I'm so sorry you are going through this!" She just gets right on my level. No shame! No advice that isn't going to work. You'd be surprised by the things people have told me to do. The worst thing I have ever done is give in to peer pressure from critics and ignore what I knew was best for my child. It never goes well. Then I'd run home to call Crystal, and she'd say, "I could have told you not to do that?"

I don't want advice unless you have been where I've been and have the scars to prove it! Like my friend John Blue always says, "Never trust a man without a limp." He's been through something. He knows your pain. He's fought his battles, wrestled with God, and is wiser for it. This is my friend Crystal. Her limp is beautiful, and it helped us find each other—a treasure among the common!

There is a passage in the Bible that has helped me guard my heart as I find my parenting tribe: "Do not throw your pearls to pigs. If you do, they may trample them under their feet and turn and tear you to pieces." (Matthew 7:6)

The verse is talking about preaching the gospel to those who aren't ready to hear it. But whenever I read it, I think about bearing my soul or telling my story to people who don't get it. It's like handing my baby to someone reckless. I immediately regret it and want to say, "Never mind! Never mind! Give him back, please. You're going to hurt him!"

That's how my emotions feel when I bear my soul to the wrong person. I have found myself feeling that way from time to time in the presence of certain friends as it related to my strong-willed children. It wasn't so much that they didn't care about my parenting woes, but they didn't get the depth of what I was going through. In a vulnerable moment, I confided in one particular friend that my son had yelled, "I hate you and wish you had never been born!" She seemed so shocked. She told me her child had never done that, and I had a *huge* problem on my hands. (Ya think?) It made me feel ashamed. It made me retreat, and, as the Scripture says, my fragile feelings felt "trampled under her feet."

Another time at lunch with friends, I confided in them about the time my son made me so mad that I pulled over, kicked him out, and drove around the block. It was not my best moment. I watched as they gave each other "side-eyes," seemingly forming judgments. It's not their fault. Again, I have learned that if they don't have a difficult or strong-willed child, they won't understand, they don't have experiences to draw from or know what to say.

Seek out those who *do* get it, who *have been there* or are *currently* in the trenches with you. Pray to find them. You could even put some feelers out. But please don't retreat and withdraw because of the few who unintentionally hurt you. The enemy wants to get you alone, so he can whisper his lies in your ear and pick you off. The Bible says, "Your enemy, the devil prowls around like a roaring lion looking for someone to devour!" (1 Peter 5:8) Don't be devoured by the enemy! Go find your people because there is strength in numbers. One of my favorite verses in the Bible reminds us that two are better than one, and three—well, three is even better (Yay!):

> Two are better than one, because they have a good return for their labor: if either of them falls down,

one can help the other up. But pity anyone who falls and has no one to help them up. Also, if two lie down together, they will keep warm. But how can one keep warm alone? Though one may be overpowered, two can defend themselves. A cord of three strands is not quickly broken. (Ecclesiastes 4:9-12)

I recently did a Bible study by Priscilla Shire. If you haven't ever done her studies, they are phenomenal. This one was on the armor of God. She talked about Roman soldiers and the purpose of their big, heavy shields. When they were under fierce attack from the enemy, one would yell, "Turtle!" They would then put their shields up in the air to form a turtle shell to protect each other. Now those are the kind of friends I'm talking about! They have your back, know what a fierce battle you are fighting, and are committed to your success and livelihood. They encourage one another, laugh together, offer wisdom and insight, and have compassion and your best interest at heart. I pray that you find each other and become a force to be reckoned with.

Keep trying, keep swinging, keep putting yourself out there. It is worth being vulnerable. I promise you, the right people are out there. People like Crystal, who pray while you drag umbrellas out of the pool, and like Paula who pour coffee and commiserates. People like Chris who fight for your kiddos as if they were their own and proclaim the "Year of Jubilee" over your life. Find friends like Jodi who bring comfort food and speak calmly when you are frantic and April who come running when you call. Find a friend like Julia who has your back and send up a Hallelujah when needed, and like Suzanne who remind you of the powerful God you serve—who began a good work in you and will be faithful to complete it.

This is one badass "Ninja-Turtle" formation if you ask me! I'm getting emotional just writing about them. Just try to stop us! The Bible says in Psalm 27:13 NASB, "I would have despaired unless I had believed that I would see the goodness of the Lord in the land of the living." This is that. This is the land of the living!

Some of these gals have been here from the very beginning, and others I found along the way: in a dance class, at the park, in a preschool room, or in a small group. A deep friendship is formed when you say, "Oh my gosh, you too? I thought I was the only one." Some took years. Some were instant. God gives you *what* you need and *who* you need right *when* you need it. Be open. Be vulnerable. They are out there waiting for you, and they need you as much as you need them. My prayer is that in them you will find a safe place where your heart is cherished and covered by their shields of faith, and your weary arms will be held up so that you may be victorious in battle.

25

THE TRIBE RIGHT
UNDER YOUR NOSE

Have you ever attempted to hang a piece of artwork in just the right spot? My husband prefers to use that level with the bubble in the middle. You know the one; it floats a little to the left, then a little to the right, and rarely do we get it right on the first try. But, oh, how sweet it is when we see it hovering right in the middle. It is a cause for a great celebration! Admittedly, I don't always have the patience to use the level. I prefer to put multiple holes in the wall and pray that the artwork will graciously cover them. (This is the basic difference between my husband and me in just about every area of life.)

This is also similar to the delicate balancing act I do between serious parenting and fun-loving friendship with my children. I know "they" say your child needs a parent, not a friend. But *I* dare say your child needs both. Of course, I'm not out here partying with minors or aiding and abetting their poor choices, but I do believe there is value in cultivating a healthy friendship with your children. I've worked hard over the years to do just that in the name of capturing their hearts. I call it my sweet spot. I love these people so much, and I want to share my whole heart with them. We are wired for relationships. By showing my fun side and vulnerable side, I allow them the space to show theirs.

It can get a little tricky when you have to pull back and put on your "disciplinarian hat." It can feel one-sided at times, especially when your children are little. But it's worth it to me to keep trying to find that perfect bubble, to build bonds, to make memories, and to see them laugh and let loose with us and not just be part of the background of our lives. Some people live such separate lives from their kids—contrary to what we are striving for here. Whether they are strong-willed or not, your kids need to know they are wanted and valued by you.

My daughter Sam would sometimes visit the homes of her classmates only to return saying, "I wondered if her family even liked each other because no one was hanging out in the kitchen spending time together." One day when Rebekah was in middle school, I received the sweetest text from her shortly after she boarded the bus saying, "Just sat next to a girl who told me she hated her mom!" (I took it all with a grain of salt because I've been there before.) This encounter made Rebekah sad. She said, "Can you even imagine? Love you, Mom!"

"Love you too, Bekah!"

In *Shepherding a Child's Heart,* Tedd Tripp writes about the importance of investing in our children and cautions us about getting too busy and pushing them away.[1]

"Get out of the kitchen!" we say.

"Get out of my office!"

"Just get in the car. We're late!"

"Be quiet. I'm on the phone!"

And then when they are older, we wonder why they don't "gather 'round the kitchen."

Remember Chad's colleague? Make your friends before you need them. Maybe here we could say, "Cultivate your relationships while you have them to cultivate." Work on them while your kids are still a captive audience in your home and under your roof, and you will find deep, meaningful relationships that transcend the teen years and last a lifetime—a homegrown tribe of sorts. My family does love to be together, but it's something I've intentionally worked at over the years.

Try speaking their love language. Most children's love language is quality time. In a big, busy family, one-on-one quality time is especially important. When my girls were little, I found my sweet spot playing dress-up and playing with Barbies and going on bike rides and baking (lots of baking). On the go and during the fun is where friendships are forged. As they got older, spending time together became the norm.

"Wanna run errands with me?"

"Sure! Do we have time to pop into that coffee shop?"

Your kids need to know you like them. Life is so hard, and people can be harsh. Be a soft, safe place for them to land. For Adam, it was Legos and basketball. You have no idea how much basketball I have played. Maybe this is why professional athletes thank their moms when they are on TV.

For David, it was reading and gardening. While reading one night he confided in me that fourth grade was hard, and kids were being mean to him. Then he asked me if I would come to lunch. The Elementary school lunchroom is not my favorite place to be. But on this day I sat with my son as we ate sub sandwiches and drank smoothies from Thundercloud, and I pretended he was the only kid in the room. It was like we were on a date, and his stories were fascinating. I hung on his every word. I watched his heart fill with confidence and pride and joy. Then I watched him skip back to the fourth-grade classroom. Call it what you want. I call it friendship! My boy needed a friend. I desire to lift my children's spirits, just like I would for any friend.

I remember an episode of *Friends* where Chandler, recalling his childhood traumas, was having a tough time on Thanksgiving. Monica wanted to cheer him up, so she put the whole raw turkey on her head and did a shimmy dance for him. (Go look it up. It's hilarious and heartwarming!)

Anything for a friend!

Anything for a smile!

This is how I feel.

One day years ago when Samantha came home burdened over some middle school drama, I turned on Taylor Swift's song, "Shake It Off," and proceeded to dance around the kitchen for her. I have many talents, but dancing is not one of them, so I thought surely this would improve her mood. She did not budge for 3 minutes of a song that is 3 minutes and 39 seconds long, but she did eventually crack a smile. Maybe she smiled because I was huffing and puffing (that's a long song!) or maybe because she had a friend who noticed and cared.

This is what I do for my people. I'd do it for you! I'm going to do it for them. It's why we dress up for Halloween, have board game night, and go to *all* of the games—*all—of—them!* Who wants to look into the stands and see no one? Who wants to bring their problem into the kitchen and find it empty and stark? All the action happens in the kitchen at my house. I have spent years purposely stationing myself there just in case. I made myself available with an ear and a smile and a cookie. I was saying, "You can tell me anything! I'm here for you!"

In full disclosure, my family has a ruthless streak where we make fun of each other when we flub our words or have an awkward social interaction out in public. Nothing goes unnoticed, and we will mercilessly take each other out in a basketball or board game. We even invite prospective suitors to join us in our unforgivingly competitive events—so be forewarned! It's like running a gauntlet. But there is a tribal loyalty behind it all, a deep foundation of trust and respect. We will love you fiercely with hearts the size of Texas.

Sometimes I think the loyalty and kindness I see in my family is genetic. The competitive edge and the social awkwardness are, so it's safe to assume the rest is too. But they can also be taught and should always be modeled in your home. To me, it's the difference between a house and a home. You can be people who *have* to live together or people who enjoy each other's friendship. Again, we are not perfect, but striving toward it!

One particular fall night a few years ago, we were busy in the grind of life with our heads down, tired from too many bad days. I was determined to stop the crazy train and love on my people. It was similar to when you haven't seen a friend in a while, and you stop and think, *Ya know, I ought to call her.* It's that. I declared it "clean out the fridge night." It's Samantha's favorite type of dinner. I think it feels like community to her. We made salads out of everything we could find. I made quesadillas out of tortillas that were starting to look more like Frisbees, and Adam concocted an odd-tasting smoothie that we all agreed just needed more honey. (Most things just need more honey.)

We put the smoothies in blue goblets and took everything outside to the back patio sans iPhones (but made sure to record the football game because we are not savages). We talked about everything and nothing. And we laughed loud and hard. (Laughter is the best medicine.)

David reminded us that it is bad luck if you don't clink glasses with *everyone* at your table during a toast, so everyone awkwardly touched the glass of everyone else at the table with a different greeting.

"Salutations!"

"Cheers!"

"Good day!"

The awkward clinking was music to my ears. Adam even showed us a Mexican hat dance he learned in music class while the girls and I hummed "La Cucaracha." This is way better than eating in the car, eating in shifts like ships passing in the night, or shushing kids at a stuffy boring restaurant. Small efforts make for big memories!

"To friendship!" I said, raising my glass.

"To friendship!" they said, and the clinking began again.

A change of scenery, blue goblets, undivided attention, and laughter—it is so life-giving. I watched tired students shake off the blues of the day and the weight of the world, if only for an hour.

I love when these moments happen organically, but I also intentionally look for them. I try to fan the flame when they appear. We are loud and exhausting. We leave a big wake. I would say seventy percent of the fun family things we *try* to plan end in tears. These organic pop-up moments, though, seem to be our jam. My husband and I will look at each other in a precious moment like this with a twinkle in our eyes as if we are seeing a rare bird in its natural habitat. Don't move or the moment will be lost.

That night our children went to bed happy and woke up strengthened by the reprieve. I was equally strengthened by the reprieve. Do you have those times? Watch for them and gently fan the flame.

Cultivating a friendship with your child can be tricky, especially with a difficult or strong-willed child. Oh, how deeply I know this! They can ruin the moment, the day, the holiday season, your life! But what choice do you have if you are in it for the long haul? You can stay bitter and distant, or you can forgive. Get back in there, and try to make some memories. Dr. John Townsend in his book

Who's Pushing Your Buttons says, "Love is not satisfied with the quiet death of two souls that are externally connected but internally alienated from each other."[2] The key is *daily* forgiveness. Don't grow so weary with your child that you become bitter. Remember, you are the adult. Try to keep your heart soft towards them so these moments have soil to grow and flourish.

Give everything you've got to these sweet precious babies. No one knows them like you do. No one can love them like you can. Close the doors, sing, dance, and let them know they have your heart, and, in turn, they will give you theirs.

Currently, my daughters are twenty-one and nineteen, and the boys are fifteen and fourteen, and I consider them my tribe—my people. My girls are among my very best friends. We all long to be together as often as possible, and we have the best time when we are together. We communicate daily through memes, texts, and facetime. Our group messages and inside jokes are my absolute favorite. We even have a six-person group text entitled "Squad." Someone changes the name from time to time, and it's something I look forward to. I'm going to go change it to "My Tribe" or "Crazy Train" or "People I Can't Get Enough Of"!

26

WALK WITH THE WISE

In 2008, we left the charismatic, spirit-filled church we had attended for roughly eight years here in Austin as it was crumbling down around us. Leaving was bittersweet because I met so many wonderful friends there and watched as God scattered a majority of them around the globe. I was left fostering some long-distance relationships as we found a new church home at a wonderful Baptist church right by our neighborhood. Chad and I laugh now because we didn't know much about denominations at the time, and we are the farthest thing from Baptist. I knew the Lutheran church I grew up in and the charismatic church I just left, and that was about it. We didn't even know our new little home was a Baptist church until we were well into membership classes. But what we did know was that we loved the people.

We took our kiddos to vacation Bible school there for years before ever attending. It was super convenient and super fun, and they had a little carnival on the last night that was the highlight of the week for both kids and parents. The first time we attended, I arrived on the scene visibly overwhelmed with my two little girls by my side and my baby boys locked and loaded in the double stroller. Chad was planning to meet me there but was running late, so I was relieved to see smiling faces and helpful volunteers. A man brought me a soda and a hot dog and offered me a chair in the shade while a lovely teenage girl took my kids for pony rides.

My soul was weary from parenting, and a long season of church politics and spiritual battles had left me leery of "church folk." But here, everyone was so kind, and I felt the goodness of God. To my surprise, this was a normal occurrence and not just an exception to the rule. This church and its community restored my faith in humanity and reminded me that "church folk" can be good, and that the body of Christ is meant to be a blessing. Here I went to Sunday school, women's Bible study, and parenting classes, and sent my kiddos to camp.

When my daughter became very sick, new friends sent comforting emails and texts. They brought food, movies, books, and much appreciated advice and wisdom. Many offered to babysit my little ones, cook, clean, and even drive carpools. And they prayed.

Community done right is a powerful thing. The book of Acts paints a lovely picture of what a healthy community looked like in the church's early formation:

> They devoted themselves to the apostles' teaching and to fellowship, to the breaking of bread and to prayer. Everyone was filled with awe at the many wonders and signs performed by the apostles. All the believers were together and had everything in common. They sold property and possessions to give to anyone who had need. Every day they continued to meet together in the temple courts. They broke

bread in their homes and ate together with glad and sincere hearts, praising God, and enjoying the favor of all the people. And the Lord added to their number daily those who were being saved. (Acts 2:42-47)

Jesus reaching out through others to help us was beautiful to behold. There was no reason on earth that I should have felt so calm and full of faith in that season. Nothing had immediately changed about my daughter's condition except for faithful people, selflessly gathered around praying for her, loving on us, and meeting our needs. I watched my daughter heal from the inside out! And do you know what? So did I because of this community.

No church is perfect! If you are looking for the perfect church, you won't find it because they are filled with imperfect people like you and me. But there are some fabulous churches out there, following the example of the early church and truly devoted to one another's well-being.

If you have lost faith in the local church or maybe never seen the need for it, may I encourage you to find a healthy local church and lean into it during this season? When you feel weary from the battle, when you want to isolate yourself, please don't. Do what you need to do to get to church. Go on a Saturday night if that works better. Find one with a stellar, grace-giving children's church, drop your kids off, and run! Run into the sanctuary into the arms of Jesus to worship in a Bible study. You have so much to gain by becoming part of a community that is bigger than just your four walls that are consuming you with parenting struggles.

Join a small group.

Go on a mission trip.

Take part in a vacation Bible school.

Sing in the choir.

You have so much to *offer* as well. The body of Christ needs you, your gifts, and your talents (when you are ready!). Sometimes you need to just go to church to get spiritually fed, soak up the presence of the Lord. Then go home and take a big nap! Right? Maybe that's all you have the bandwidth for. I get that. For a while when we were first at the Baptist church, we laid low like we were in a witness protection program. We were thinking, *Don't let anyone know that we are seasoned church leaders.* Slowly but surely, we began to engage in our community on a more active level. You go at your own pace. But do go!

My prayer is that you would quickly come alive again in the right environment. May you begin to do some of the things you used to do or long to do, such as running, cooking, dancing, shopping, laughing, eating, going to movies, or listening to music. Do them alongside some fantastic people from your local church. Sometimes we forget that we are actual people who had actual interests and lives before we had kids.

Over the years I've gone to women's groups (and even hosted some. God bless me!) where we'd go around to introduce ourselves by saying, "Hi! I'm Tami, and I am married to Chad. We have four children, and their names are…" But there is so much more to us isn't there? It's nice to step away from that for a while and get to know other people who make up the body of Christ and see what else we have in common (along with Jesus). Why not present ourselves by saying something like, "Hello! My name is Tami. I love to run, cook, read, and listen to country music. I love Jesus and his Word, and I love to teach others about him." I can talk a little bit about me, a little bit about the gifts and talents I'm bringing, and about this little fun fact here: "Oh yeah, I also have these crazy kids."

Realize that you have unique qualities that are useful to the body of Christ, your community, and the world. Serving with your gifts and talents is a great way to take your mind off your woes. Remember, there is more to you than being a mom, more to you than your strong-willed child. You will come away refreshed and recharged, and so will others, resulting—as we see in the book of Acts—in an even bigger community. (Hooray!) This is what the church has been to me!

Back when I first gave my life to Christ, while I was safely tucked away in the Baptist church, and now serving here at Renovate Church in Leander, Texas, I've met the most amazing people. They have poured such godly wisdom into me, and I am eternally grateful. I've learned how to pray, worship, study the Bible, serve, and love my neighbor. I've learned how to endure trials, forgive, be a better wife and friend, and, yes, be a better parent.

I long to be with friends who speak the truth about God's Word, his character, and his faithfulness and spur me on to be more Christ-like. I want to go from glory to glory and strength to strength as the Bible tells us:

Not that I have already obtained all this, or have already arrived at my goal, but I press on to take hold of that for which Christ Jesus took hold of me. Brothers and sisters, I do not consider myself yet to have taken hold of it. But one thing I do: Forgetting what is behind and straining toward what is ahead, I press on toward the goal to win the prize for which God has called me heavenward in Christ Jesus. (Philippians 3:12-14)

But that takes others. That takes wise men and women running alongside me! I am eternally grateful to God for leading me to my little Baptist church, for healing my heart, and for restoring my faith in community and the local church. I pray that you find the same.

PART 6

YOU'VE GOT THIS

Let us not become weary in doing good, for at the proper time, we will reap a harvest if we do not give up.

Galatians 6:9

27

YOU ARE A SUPERHERO

Once upon a time in a church foyer, far, far away, I overheard a friend say to my husband, "I don't know how your wife does it, man." Statements like that used to always offend me. I felt like what he wanted to say was "I don't know *why* you had all these crazy kids, and it's clear your wife doesn't know what she is doing!" But then he said, "She must be wearing a cape under there!" which struck me funny because he and his wife also had four children, and she seemed to be killing it! Perhaps he just knew a superhero when he saw one. What might have warranted his comments was that my two young boys *were running around* like wild animals that morning. I would describe it as a play date gone bad with no one coming to pick up the other kid anytime soon.

I chose to take it as a compliment, but, of course, under my breath, I said to myself, "Yeah, *I wish* I had a cape on under here!" Wouldn't that be great if I could channel some sort of higher power in my moments of crisis like when Clark Kent saw danger and dashed into a phone booth emerging as Superman, or when David Banner had enough of being "mister nice guy" and transformed into the Incredible Hulk? I wished I had *something* or *someone* greater than my human abilities to help me out. I wanted some kind of supernatural strength to tap into when the world seemed to be throwing kryptonite at me.

It's fun to daydream about super nannies and superheroes for a bit, but the reality is that we *do* have a higher power readily available in Christ. And it is the answer I give when someone asks me how I do it. When you are feeling less than heroic, remind yourself of these truths:

1. **God is your source of power!** There were times when I thought I couldn't possibly make it through the days and the seasons of this lovely parenting journey. But the Bible tells me that with God all things are possible! So, I clung to God and asked him to help me do the impossible. The Lord hears us when we cry out to him. Not only does he bring rest and strength, but he brings his supernatural power. It's available through the Holy Spirit that lives in every Christian.[1]

It's like finding and hitting the turbo boost button on a new car. Oh, it went fast before, but now it's a whole new level of power! And with it comes a calm confidence, not unlike when superheroes realize what their supernatural transformation has now made possible. When God empowers you, there is nothing you can't do.

How did Daniel interpret dreams or Peter walk on water? How did the early Christian church, full of unpopular, persecuted, and maligned individuals, persevere and become the official religion of the Roman Empire? Every single one of the apostles of Christ (and Daniel too) was able to perform miracles (supernatural events) through the power of Christ in them, and, by the way, so can you!

Ask him to demonstrate his power in your weakness.[2] You are already one strong-willed mama out here getting it done, just reach down (or should I say up?) and hit that turbo boost!

2. God is your source of strength! When you are exhausted physically, mentally, and emotionally, and you feel weak and weary from the battle, call upon the Lord and ask him to give you strength. *He* wants to shoulder your burden. The Bible tells us in 2 Corinthians that when we are weak is actually when we are strong. That is when his power is on display. It's like asking your dad or your husband or someone stronger than you are to carry your heavy load. They get to bless you and show off their strength, and you get to rest. (It's another win-win situation!)

Jesus says in the book of Matthew, "Come to Me, all you who are weary and burdened, and I will give you rest." And Peter instructs us to "cast your cares upon the Lord because he cares for you." I always envision myself saying, "Ok, you asked for it!" and throwing a surprisingly oversized sack of burdens His way. But the Lord is not surprised. He delights in helping us. Weakness is not bad. It's just a reminder that we need God and a reminder of where true strength comes from.[3]

I am reminded of the story of Elijah in the Old Testament. Elijah was running for his life and was weary and tired from his battles. He cried out, "I've had enough Lord!" Then he fell asleep under a tree. When he awoke an angel of the Lord had made him cake. Then he took another nap. When he awoke, there was more food provided by angels, and the Bible says he was strengthened for his journey. Isn't that the best story?[4]

God wants to give you strength for your journey. Sometimes he swoops in like a superhero to lift your heavy burdens, and sometimes you need a nap and a snack. Both are from him. The Bible tells us that "Those who wait for the Lord will gain new strength. They will mount up with eagles' wings. They will run and not get tired. They will walk and not grow weary." (Isaiah 40:31) I want to rest in him so I can gain new strength. I want to run and not be tired or weary. (I also want an angel to make me a cake while I take a nap!)

3. God has given you victory over the enemy. The Bible says that you are not fighting against flesh and blood but that your struggle is against the powers of darkness and the spiritual forces of evil in the heavenly realms. Does that sound weird? It's true! There's a whole battle going on in the heavens. When you realize this truth and that your children are not the enemy (although it feels like that sometimes), you can turn your energy and prayers against the real enemy who seeks to destroy your family. Your focus will change from anger and frustration at your children to one of steadfast prayer and persistence in your faith. It is empowering to know that you serve a mighty, victorious God who helps you fight your battles.[5]

4. God prepares us for battle. The Scriptures instruct us to use some spiritual truths as weapons. God wouldn't send you into battle unprepared. Use things like truth as a belt around your waist, righteousness like a breastplate, peace under your feet like shoes, and faith like a shield to protect yourself from every evil thing in the world and even combat struggles in your thought life. It's a fascinating passage of scripture that warrants reading when you find the time. Yes, there is a war going on, my friend—against you, your precious children, and their future. But God has made you strong and mighty! (Ephesians 6:10-18)

The Bible is chock full of victory stories. It has been a source of inspiration and power for me in some of my darkest hours, and I pray it can be that for you as well. God is for you! He is your ever-present help in times of trouble. He is better than the Supernanny, Incredible Hulk and Superman rolled into one. And by His strength and through His power and grace, so are we!

28

GOD SEES YOU

Alone in the solace of my shower one night, I raised my fists to God as I have done countless times in the past. The shower is my quiet confessional, the place where I talk to God and he talks to me. Perhaps there I am vulnerable with nothing to hide and nowhere to run, or maybe it's the white noise of the water that drowns out everything around me. It's not the only place I hear God, but it is where I am honest with him.

I have raised my fists in frustration and anger as well as impatience before, but this night I raised my fists to God in a victorious "Yes!" Yes, because I see answers to my prayers, and I see progress with my son! I see fewer outbursts, fewer struggles, and more smiles. There is laughter and peace in my home. We seem to have reached a plateau of sorts, and I am letting my soul revel in the victory here in my shower.

Yes!

We did this!

God, *you* did this!

You answered my prayers, and *You—see—me!*

Yes! I raised my fists in victory, the same way David "fist-pumped" us from the court when he scored his very first points in basketball, or when Rebekah got that perfect hit in volleyball. From the stands, we fist pumped back with the most satisfying, "Yes!" and victorious laughter because we knew the back story. We were saying, "I've seen your faithfulness, blood, sweat, and tears, and my soul rejoices with yours! I see you!"

Sometimes my fists are raised in utter surrender to and dependence on God. Parenting is hard. Relationships are hard. Life is hard. There are days I've felt very alone and wondered if he was even out there. Had he heard my prayers? Did he even care?

"Answer me! Why don't you answer? I'm dyin' here!"

But deep in my spirit, I knew he saw me and was moving in my life. I could see the pieces of my mess coming together. I could see the answers to my prayers, practical prayers that I handed over to him. These deep soul prayers that I dared to utter in the wee hours of the night when all hope seemed lost were neither forgotten nor ignored.

Because he sees me, I felt him helping me, carrying me, and doing for me when I was weary. Strengthening me when I felt weak, supporting me when it seemed I was all alone, this is what it feels like to be in the will of God. I was terrified and courageous at the same time, weak and also strong. There was, all of a sudden, peace in the middle of my tornado. It was a calm in my whirlwind and an assurance of promises and victory.

"I see you," he said, "like I saw you when you were little, when you were fifteen, nineteen, twenty-four, and thirty. And I see you now. I saw the tears and the doubts and the sleepless nights. I see you. I love you. I am for you."

Dear friends, he cares for you and loves you too! he sees you in the middle of the night, before the kids rise, and in your car. And, yes, even in the shower. It's okay to show your emotions, anger, frustration, and even doubt. He sees you. He already knows. He created you. Allow yourself to *let* him see you! Let him help you and bring you victory. He is an ever-present help in times of trouble, and his invitation awaits:

> All the days ordained for me were written in your book before one of them came to be. How precious to me are your thoughts, God! How vast is the sum of them! Were I to count them, they would outnumber the grains of sand...

Psalm 139:16b–18b

29

STAY IN THE RING

Recently, I listened to my young, teenage son call his grandma on the phone. He talked about his day, his sports, and his academic success with pride in his voice—without my prompting. He asked her about her day and seemed to really care. She asked a few times if he was sick or maybe tired because his voice sounded different to her. He said, "No, Grandma. I'm just getting older." They get older. They really do!

I know it doesn't seem like they ever will. The toddler and elementary days seem to be never-ending, like the movie Groundhog Day where the same day is lived over and over again. The morning clashes, lunchtime tantrums, naptime and bedtime struggles—there seems to be something to battle every hour on the hour when they are little. Some days I forget how hard that was even though it wasn't that long ago. I think God helps us forget, similar to how we forget the pain of childbirth. It's probably so we can continue to love them through it all. I remember crying a lot, wondering what I did to deserve such around-the-clock torture. While crying into the armchair in my room, I would collapse before getting four hours of sleep, only to get up and repeat the cycle again and again—until one day it changed.

I never really thought it would change, but it did. My husband and I high-fived each other about it the other night—secretly, under the covers, so as not to jinx it. My son used to be so hard to grab, so hard to catch, so uninterested in connecting with us. He was so hard to slow down, and you could forget ever trying to hug him. These days he moves slower, asks my advice, and speaks freely about what's on his mind and his heart. He offers hugs often, and he gets his feelings hurt if I watch "our favorite shows" without him. Dare I say, we are friends? Don't get me wrong, he is still a teen! He grunts and groans, and his moods swing, and his feet stink to high heaven.

What used to be just glimpses into the future are becoming long stretches of reality that we hope will turn into the new norm. It's like a long romantic date with your spouse, in the sense that you know you can't live forever in that moment, but you savor it and are reminded why you love him. It's like looking at a sleeping toddler at the end of a very long day, praying and sensing all the potential. I am savoring the moments and sensing the potential. I cried morning and night, praying that God would calm the storm inside this strong-willed boy and give me the strength to face another day. Our God is faithful!

My house has been a training ground for so long and still is, in a sense. I am still in the thick of training young men, but I sense a shift has been taking place. These days it feels more like a launching pad. The years of tears and bone-tired nights are gone, and there is laughter and lingering in my kitchen. I feel like I have room to breathe. I white-knuckled life for many years, but these days I can loosen my grip.

Do you feel this way?

Do you pray and cry and forget to breathe?

Are you holding on for dear life?

I see you, and I understand.

They do grow up!

It does get better!

Things will begin to shift and change, and your prayers and tears are not in vain. Every ounce of energy and love you pour out for these little ones makes a difference. It adds up and is tucked away somewhere in there, and you *will* have a return on your investment if you invest wisely into your little bundle of miraculous frustration.

There is something to be celebrated when they crawl or walk, when they can tie their shoes, buckle their seatbelt, and even make their own food. (All of that, yes!) But when you see them grow spiritually or emotionally in those areas you prayed for—and wondered, *Do they just grow out of it? Please say they just grow out of it*—there will be rejoicing deep in your soul because you have done well shaping them and molding them to the glory of God.

Good job, Mama! Well done!

By now you know that my children are far from perfect. Heck, just this morning my boys threw a pile of mismatched socks violently at each other before running out the door. I found them strewn about by the toaster and coffee pot. There is work to be done here on my launching pad, but I am choosing to celebrate the fact that it was easier to clean up socks than, say, baby food or random Lego pieces or to pull patio furniture out of my pool. We will have long forgotten about the socks by this afternoon. I am rejoicing in the evolution of the soul, if you will, the fruit of growing pains, the blossoming of that which I planted long ago, wondering if it was perhaps sown in vain.

You are not sowing in vain!

That stinky, ornery, little toddler who screams, "No!" and throws poop, will turn out to be a kind-hearted human being with a good conscience, whom you like to be with! Don't be surprised if he likes to be with you too. That's the best part! Stay in the ring, mamas. Stay—in—the—ring!

30

CELEBRATE GROWTH

Years ago, during a trying time of sickness for my youngest daughter, I took it upon myself to plant a garden. I think I needed a happy distraction, or maybe I needed to feel the power and control to create life. Either way, I planted a garden. There was a part of me that thought it would be fun and a part of me that thought it might be an epic failure. My mom, as well as my mother-in-law, both have the greenest thumbs in town, but, historically, I do not. I've been known to kill a poinsettia in just a week. But much to my surprise, my garden was a success. It even began to thrive and grow into something beautiful and lush.

I had more big, red, juicy tomatoes than I knew what to do with, and I would carry dozens of cherry tomatoes around in my aprons, declaring myself a farmer. My garden yielded the freshest crop of crisp cucumbers I have ever tasted and even some humble, little honeydews. At my mom's advice, all along the edges, I planted some bright, yellow marigolds that apparently keep away the bees and mosquitos, and just for kicks, we carelessly scattered sunflower seeds throughout. They grew surprisingly fast and tall. So tall that we could see the vibrant, yellow petals greeting us each morning from the kitchen window. I was very proud of myself, and the garden was a welcome distraction for me in that season.

As spring turned to summer and my daughter grew stronger, my attention was drawn to my youngest son, David. There is always something and someone to tend to. Isn't there? He was just seven and had had a rough school year, and no one was happier to see summer than he. It's tough being little sometimes, and I could sense he needed my attention. In my heart, I declared it "the rebuilding of Dave." I wanted to breathe life into him, see his smile and his wit come alive again as his body and soul soaked in the summer sun. We all need that sometimes.

I invited him to read his Bible with me in the mornings and then come tend to our garden that was still thriving. Every morning I took my coffee, and David followed me as we headed out to see what there was to see. We watered, checked for tomato worms and bunny bites, and "changers" as David liked to call them. Changers were anything that grew overnight.

The excitement on his face was priceless when he would see last night's green tomato now changed to orange or the last night's orange tomatoes now gone. My brave gardening partner would pull and pull and pull at a juicy, green, tomato worm until it gave up the battle and was plucked from the branch, and he would squash it to smithereens. (Gross little suckers!) Then sometimes we would just sit and behold God's creation. He has always been deep beyond his years. Even back then, David would say things that would blow me away and melt my heart at the same time. A few of our conversations that summer started like this:

"Just take a deep breath, Mom, and look at all God has created for us! We are like his plants in his garden, and he watches over us like we are watching over ours."

"I feel like a changer Mom! I grow overnight too!"

"This is our 'thing' together, Mom. I Love you!"

I wonder if he knew about the amount of work I'd put in behind the scenes—the fertilizer and insecticide spray I used, how I googled "how to start a garden" and "what to do when your plants won't grow" and "how to get rid of bunnies" and "what is blight?" Did he recall that no one else but me liked tomatoes or cucumbers? Not even him! But it was our *thing*. In that season my son was growing and laughing and thriving. And that is what mattered. *That* was my harvest!

I love how life imitates life. I wish I could google "how to grow thriving children" and get a simple answer. The truth is, much like gardening, we encounter so many variables while parenting. You know what you *intended* to do, what you *thought* you sowed, so you scratch your head and go back to the drawing board, warding off hazardous enemies, pruning and feeding, watering and weeding, building a hedge around your precious seeds while looking desperately for "change and growth." You might wonder what happened to the fruit you saw yesterday. It seems gone now. God sees what you sowed, and he is well able to bring about growth. *He* will bring the harvest. Our job is to sow in faith. You are not alone, and you are not sowing in vain.

So much good came out of tending the garden with my sweet baby boy that summer. I am so glad that he chose to join me every morning. We enjoyed God's creation together and pondered life's mysteries. It was added value for me one morning when Adam randomly came and sat with us. Up until now, he had been uninterested in our "dumb garden," which was fine with us. We were enjoying our time together. But now we made room for Adam. He was tan from the summer sun and seemed to be growing as fast as the sunflowers. He sat quietly by my side, unimpressed perhaps but quietly sitting with us nonetheless. Everyone was welcome in my garden.

A hummingbird came and lingered by the marigolds as David and I silently communicated our enthusiasm to each other with just our eyes, not wanting to scare it away, not wanting the moment to fade. I've made those eyes at my husband before when we witnessed the kids arbitrarily getting along or performing a secret act of kindness, as if to say, "Shh, don't jinx it!"

"Hummingbirds are good luck, ya know," Adam said, loudly and unimpressed as if he'd seen it a thousand times.

"I think that's God telling us we are doing a good job, Mom!" David said.

"I think you are right, David," I said, "We are doing a great job!"

We found a little spot to plant something new—pumpkins! I've heard they are hard to grow. There's always something to tend to. Isn't there? The harvest should be plentiful.

31

DON'T BLINK

As I walked out of the orthodontist office with Adam, who was seven at the time, I offered him my hand. He smiled up at me and carefully put his hand in mine. It felt warm and familiar, fitting like the last piece of a hard puzzle. I welcomed the kindness and compliance. I have held his hand a million times over the years, but that day it felt particularly good. We looked at each other and smiled. He even skipped a bit. *At what point,* I thought to myself, *is it no longer okay to hold hands with your mom and skip?* I hope never!

There were times when I had to force him to hold my hand during a lesson in obedience or a practical act of safety. That day we held hands because we loved each other. It felt like my hard work and prayers were finally beginning to pay off. We've had highs and lows since that day, but I relished the way our hands fit together like our hearts, knowing there would be a day where he wouldn't want to hold my hand anymore. That day would come too soon.

That morning as I fixed his hair in the mirror, I noticed that the top of Adam's head had moved from chest level to right under my chin. *How is this possible?* I thought, *This is my firstborn son, with his huge puppy feet and ironclad will, who loves basketball and Legos—my son, who the doctors said was an impossible idea, who we fought for, who then gave us hell for so many years! He has a heart and an energy level the size of Texas and wears me out daily. How had he grown up so fast and become a young man right before my eyes?*

It felt as if years of heart-wrenching emotions, prayer, and hard work on *both* our parts came together at that moment, in the mirror and our hands. I relished the moment. My heart was bursting, and I could feel the grace and goodness of God, his pleasure and approval. As if he was saying, "Good job, Mama! Good job." It's important to pause and notice these moments and celebrate them. They are glimpses of growth and progress and hope. It's evidence of God's faithful hand in your midst to sustain you.

My son is now fifteen and towers over me at six foot three and growing. He still loves basketball (though Legos are long a thing of the past) and he *has* been known to hold my hand from time to time. *His* chin now rests on *my* head. And the will—it's still ironclad folks. We even butted heads pretty intensely last night, but these days those incidences are few and far between. There is something in our hearts that races to reconcile, that won't let things get out of hand or last too long. With an unspoken understanding of where we've been and just how far we've come, I soften, and he softens. And our hearts fit together once again like our hands did that day. The progress we've made is not lost on either of us. I'm proud of the strong-willed young man he has become, and I'm proud of the strong-willed mama I've become as well.

32

THERE IS A LIGHT AT THE END OF THE TUNNEL

It was a beautiful fall night here in Austin, Texas and one of the rare peewee football seasons where my boys were on the same team. I dropped them off at practice and longed to stay at the field and watch them do their thing while I basked in the sunshine. But my girls were at home, dinner needed to be made, and my presence was needed there. It was a time in my life when I was always being pulled in five different directions and stretched so thin that no one seemed to get the best of me. At least I knew Chad would pick them up, so I headed home, started dinner, and sat down at the kitchen table to chat with my girls.

Samantha began describing the day's middle school lunchroom drama in grand detail. She has always been so social and sensitive (a lethal combo that I know too well). I offered advice that I have offered countless times, and it seemed to only scratch the surface. But then something wonderful happened. As my oldest daughter Rebekah gracefully moved about the kitchen helping with dinner, she gave the perfect advice. It poured out from deep, tender parts of her soul that *I* knew were there but were rarely seen by the casual inquirer. She recounted some "not so fun times" in middle school, times when she felt abandoned, hurt, and judged, and how it made her feel—how she never wanted anyone else to ever feel that way. She cautioned her younger sister not to judge, snub, or discard anyone but to always be inclusive and kind. "It's like Mom always says, be nice or even be neutral but *never* be negative, Sam." She continued, "It's okay to keep boundaries and be true to yourself at the same time. It just takes maturity, which most people don't have at our age."

The way she moved about the kitchen, her mannerisms, and her voice inflection reminded me of myself, except taller and with better legs. (You know, the way God intended it to be.) She told us of a friend that she made at lunch because "You should always scan the room for someone who may be lonely, and ask them to join you." The conversation continued until the boys burst on the scene, and the moment was gone. But I savored it. My heart grew three sizes that night. (Yes, like the Grinch!) To raise kind-hearted children who love each other and God and can finesse that delicate balance between soft hearts and thick skin is my absolute goal in life. We are not perfect by any means, but we are getting there. That night was good.

My daughter was just shy of sixteen at the time, just coming into her own and becoming comfortable in her own skin and personality. She is kind and wise beyond her years. There were some dark seasons, some pain and tears, and she had to learn some things the hard way. But those tough times made her who she is today. To see Rebekah now use those experiences to help her sister was a beautiful thing. To see how strong she had become because of what she'd been through gave me great hope for her younger sister, who was going through some of the same struggles. It gave me hope for the little men I was currently struggling to raise.

That week I remember needing encouragement. I wondered if I had been there enough for her, if I had said the right things ... or been too busy or too tired or stretched too thin. I remember asking God for a sign, wondering if there would ever be a light at the end of my dark tunnel. This was that sign for me. God's grace is sufficient for us, and his power is made perfect through our weaknesses. No, I couldn't be in two different places at once that night, but I was right where I needed to be. This was better than watching football practice (for sure). Look for moments like these. Thank God for moments like these! Cherish them. Celebrate them.

Keep fighting the good fight. Stay in the ring. Be strong and courageous. Lean into the grace of God and be encouraged. Rejoice when you see the fruits of your labor on display. It's evidence that your hard work will indeed pay off. Even if you think your children aren't paying attention, they are. Even if you think you've fallen short and your efforts aren't enough, it's worth persevering. There is a light at the end of your tunnel.

33

DAY BY DAY

One of the most inspirational books I've ever read is Bird by Bird by Anne LaMotte. It's a witty yet deep and honest look at the angsty writing process and how complicated it can be to sit down and put pen to paper. She encouraged me greatly when at times I felt overwhelmed by "the writer's world and its treacherous swamps." In her pages she tells this story:

> "Thirty years ago, my older brother, who was ten years old at the time, was trying to get a report on birds written that he'd had three months to write. [It] was due the next day. We were out at our family cabin in Bolinas, and he was at the kitchen table close to tears, surrounded by binder paper and pencils and unopened books on birds, immobilized by the hugeness of the task ahead. Then my father sat down beside him, put his arm around my brother's shoulder, and said, 'Bird by bird, buddy. Just take it bird by bird.'"[6]

Bird by bird, mama, just take it bird by bird.

This right here is golden, my friend! The subtitle of her lovely book is equally golden: *Some Instructions on Writing and Life.* I wish I'd have thought of that! *The Strong-Willed Mama: Some Instructions on Parenting and Life.*

You might be surrounded by diapers, sippy cups, un-opened books on parenting, and immobilized by the huge-ness of the task ahead. I know! It's why I wrote this book for you—to sit beside you, put my arm around you and say, "Day by day, my sweet friend. We will take this day by day, year by year, and, of course, child by child. And you can do this!" You've got what it takes, and you are more than qualified for the job at hand.

You could be considered an expert in the field of life! Consider all the things you've been through, fought for, and accomplished. Think of the trials God has brought you victoriously through thus far. You've survived one hundred percent of your hardest days. It was probably all preparation for this season you're in right now. You are more qualified than you give yourself credit for, and you can surely do this! Sometimes we underestimate our strength or second guess ourselves when life throws us a curveball or something new is presented—something like a strong-willed child.

I remember when my girls hit their teen years. I found myself at a new level of uncertainty. And it happened again when my boys hit puberty. (But that's another book for another time.) I recalled that I had similar experienc-es before and would simply draw from my own life expe-riences with mean girls, puppy love, lunchroom drama, PMS, and the likes. Although most of us don't remember what it feels like to be a toddler, we can all relate to the hu-man conditions of frustration, anger, exhaustion, hunger, and (uh, hmmm) wanting our way. Our children are tiny humans trying to find their way in this world, and our job is to train them up in the way they should go.

Consider your qualifications, and draw from your own life experiences to help them. When I encountered a new challenge or two on the road with my children, there was always this initial sense of panic. My natural reaction was to say, "I don't know what to do here!" But if I stopped to think, *Wait a minute! I have been here before! What worked for me?* Perhaps someone to talk to, a hug or some cookies, a day at the park, or some downtime could help. Maybe even tough love and some firm boundaries might help. A nap, prayer, or counseling could be in order. We have a wellspring of data that we can adapt to each particular child. Think about what worked for you growing up and what didn't. What do you wish someone had done or not done for you?

You were born for such a time as this! You were born for this job! Your circumstances may have been a *bit* different, but chances are the solutions are quite similar. In the book of Ecclesiastes, King Solomon searches for meaning in life and says this:

What has been will be again, what has been done will be done again. There is nothing new under the sun. (Ecc. 1:9)

A commentary I found on this passage shed this encouraging light:

> "What really changes, communication, or just the methods and speed?
> Illness or just diagnosis and treatment?

Does money change or just the form they use and
the systems.
Relationships, Politics, Sin, do not confuse methods
with essence.
It is what it is.
Whatever seems to be new, has been
around for ages."[7]

You have the answers and the solutions your child needs.
You are who your child needs. You are the one for the job.
You are enough! You can do this! You are already a strong-
willed mama with a work ethic like no other, and I know
you will stop at nothing to ensure the happiness of your
family. You work nonstop doing just that. (If moms could
clock in and clock out, we could get paid what we deserve!)

On top of everything, you are far from alone. Utilize your
tribe. They have so much wisdom and experience to offer.
I'm talking about parents, grandparents, aunts and uncles,
friends, teachers, and spouses whose past and present influences in your life have not only shaped you but given
you experiences to draw from as well. A family member or
friend can speak into your situation with a different perspective and can also be a great source of encouragement.
Sometimes friends and family know you better than you
know yourself.

You have the God of the universe on your side. He has
declared that you can do all things through Christ who
strengthens you. And with God on your side, no one can
stand against you. We are commanded to bear one another's burdens and comfort others with the comfort we

have received from God. (8) Have you received any comfort from God? That's great! Now extend that to your children.

God has promised never to leave you nor forsake you. (Deut. 31:6) You have been chosen and equipped by God for this job. You are more than qualified to raise these children and bring about transformation in your family. You are an amazing, resilient woman, full of grace and confidence, and you've got this.

Bird by bird.

Child by child.

Day by day.

You've got this, Strong-Willed Mama!

You've got this!

THE STRONG-WILLED MAMA PRAYER

Lord, thank you for my child. Thank you for making them strong and independent, full of life and energetic. Thank you for choosing me to be their mom and sovereignly pairing us together. This family was your plan and I know your plans are good; all your ways are good, and you, Lord, are good.

You are not surprised by anything, Lord. You've seen my struggles and heard my cries, and I praise you for helping me thus far; for not only sustaining me, but taking me from glory to glory and from strength to strength. I know you will continue to see me victoriously to the end.

Give me strength daily.
Give me grace daily.

Lord, let there be more of you and less of me.
Show me what you want to show me.
Teach me what you want to teach me
Transform me, and in the process transform my family.

Do a work in me.
Do a work in my child.

Bring peace and harmony to our home.
Let me feel you and see your hand at work morning,
noon, and night.
I need your presence.
We need your presence.

Strengthen my soul.
Guard my mouth.
Direct my steps.

Give me wisdom, courage, patience, and love.
Let these virtues well up within me and overflow onto my
family.
Lord, bring me support in the way of your people, and
allow me to bring comfort to others.

Lord, I declare I was created for this and I can do all
things through Jesus who strengthens me. I am more
than a conqueror.

Thank you for transforming me into one strong-willed
mama.

REFLECT & TAKE ACTION

PART 1

REFLECTION

Parenting can be difficult especially when dealing with a strong-willed child. Life in general can be hard and I suspect this is not the first (or last) difficult situation you have encountered in your lifetime. The truth is, you have survived 100 percent of your difficult days so far and you will survive this season too. Jesus said, "In this world you will have trouble." (Not MIGHT) "But take heart! I have overcome the world." (John 16:33)

And so can you!

1. What are some difficult things you overcame? During these times, did you pray and ask God to help you? If so, did it make a difference to invite him into your situation? How did you see him working?

2. Do you believe God is for you and working all things together for your good? Do you trust he will be faithful to see it through to completion? Do you believe he will do it again?

3. What difficulties are you currently facing with your strong-willed child?

ACTION

- Pray and ask God to help you. Be specific.

- Write your prayers down and believe to see them answered.

- Invite a trusted friend to stand with you in prayer.

PART 2

REFLECTION

1.   How do you feel about surprises? Does it matter if
     they're good or bad? A gift from a friend for no reason,
     a surprise party, running out of gas? What about an
     unexpected challenge? A pop quiz, or a hill to climb?

2.   On a scale of 1-10 how strong-willed do you perceive
     your child to be? Do you see the term strong-willed as
     positive or negative? What positive strengths do you see
     in your child? Have you ever been caught off guard by
     the magnitude of his or her strong will?

3.   What negative emotions or feelings come up when you
     engage in a battle of wills with your child.

     Circle all that apply.

     Frustration
     Shock
     Anger
     Shame
     Fear
     Insecurity
     Sadness
     Confusion
     Inadequacy
     Regret

Rage

Depression

Anxiety

Hopelessness

Hatred

Loneliness

Bitterness

Resentment

Are your emotions directed more at yourself, your spouse, your child, or God? All of the above?

Circle the traits below you desire to see more of in your life.

Self control

Compassion

Empathy

Sympathy

Love

Patience

Faith

Hope

Confidence

Wisdom

Supportive

Understanding

Peace

Joy

Kindness

Gentless

Flexibility

Calmness

4. How is parenting this child different than you thought
    it would be? If you have multiple children, do you
    think one specific formula or method of parenting
    should work for every child? What strengths do you
    see in yourself that can help you parent your strong-
    willed child?

ACTION

- Pray and ask God to help you replace negative emotions
  and feelings with their more positive and productive
  counterparts. Reference the list as often as you need to.

- Record your growth and celebrate your victory in
  these areas.

- Record the positive strengths you see on display in your
  child this week.

- Praise him/her for them.

PART 3

REFLECTION

1. What is your most embarrassing moment? What was the worst part? How did you handle it? Did you learn anything? Has your child ever embarrassed you in public? What was the worst part? How did you handle it? Did you learn anything?

    God certainly doesn't want to embarrass us, but he does use our circumstances to bring about growth and change. It's quite possible he is using your parenting journey to transform you.

    Why do you think that is?

2. Do you struggle with anger? What do you do to cool off?

    The presence of our negative emotions can actually lead us to Jesus, who then sets us free. "So if the Son sets you free, you will be free indeed"(John 8:36).

    Have you asked Him to set you free from anger?

3. In what other areas are you experiencing growth in this season?

    Confidence
    Strength
    Self control

Discipline
Faith
Patience
Wisdom
Unity in your marriage
Other:

There is no limit to the things God can teach us through this parenting journey, and he will use all of our experiences to change us for the better and transform us if we let him. Trust me, he wastes nothing.

ACTION

- Pray and ask God to show you what he's working on and then, get in on it!

- Notice common struggles you have with your child and purposefully offer some grace and understanding. Maybe even tell them you know how they feel and offer to pray for them.

- As you grow through what you go through, you can help them to do the same.

- Keep a journal of the things God teaches you and celebrate your family's progress and new found freedom.

PART 4

REFLECTION

There is a lot of information available about discipline. Our success is going to lie at the intersection of what works for our family and is pleasing to God.

Children crave boundaries and consistency. They also crave love and approval. A healthy home will have a balance of both. Although we can't always have perfect days, we can take steps towards having more good days than bad days. That, to me, is a win.

1.   What does a perfect day with your family look like? What sabotages a good time? What redeems a difficult day?

2.   Do you spend time studying your child to know what makes him/her tick? What is your child's Love Language? What is their "sweet spot" and "currency"?

3.   When it comes to discipline do you err on the side of grace or being too strict? Do you need to make any adjustments? What worries you about making adjustments? How might making positive changes bring transformation to your family?

4.   Does your child respond differently to grandparents or a beloved relative? Is there something you can learn

from those interactions? What does it mean to be wise as a serpent and gentle as a dove?

5. How does the notion that the strong will is a good, God-given trait change your outlook on discipline? What does it look like for you to pick your battles? How can you make your home both a safe sanctuary for the soul and a transformational training ground?

ACTION

- As you study your child and make positive adjustments to your parenting style, record how it transforms your home.

- Be mindful of what ministers to your child's soul and redeems a difficult day.

PART 5

REFLECTION

1. Have you ever confided in the wrong person? What was the experience like? How did it compare to finding, and confiding in, the right person?

2. Who do you consider your tribe? Do you consider your family your tribe? Why or why not? What about your church?

3. Do you find it hard to open up and tell people what you are going through? What are some factors that keep you from opening up? How have your closest people supported you in this season?

ACTION

- Host a big family dinner to love on your people and remind them how special they are.

- Call your tribe and tell them how life-giving they are to you!

- If you are not part of a local church, consider steps in that direction by visiting some in your area.

PART 6

REFLECTION

1. If you were a superhero, what would your superpower be?

2. Look back at all you have endured and revel in what a bad-ass you are. Remind yourself that this is all serving to make you even stronger and transform your family.

ACTION

- Write your resume for the job opening: Strong-willed mama needed to raise strong-willed children.

- Look in the mirror and tell yourself, "You've got this!"

- Call a friend and tell her, "You've got this!"

NOTES

PART 1: LET'S START AT THE VERY BEGINNING

1. Philippians 1:6, 4:3

2. Do It Again. Elevation Worship. *There is a Cloud.* Essential Music Publishing, 2017

PART 2: CONGRATULATIONS! IT'S A STRONG-WILLED CHILD!

1. Bad Boys (Theme song to "Cops") Inner Circle. *One Way.* Ian Lewis Publishing, 1987

PART 3: GROW THROUGH WHAT YOU GO THROUGH

1. Seltzer PH.D, Leon F. Evolution of Self, "Feeling Vulnerable? No Problem- Just Get Angry" *Psychology Today.* 07 Mar. 2018, https://www.psychologytoday.com/us/blog/evolution-the-self/201803/feeling-vulnerable-no-problem-just-get-angry

PART 4: FROM TANTRUMS TO TRANSFORMATION

1. Warren, Rick. "Punishment and Discipline: There is a difference" Daily Hope with Rick Warren. *Grace in the City.* 14 Nov. 2013, https://gracesinthecity.wordpress.com/2013/11/14/daily-hope-with-rick-warren-punishment-and-discipline-there-is-a-difference/

2. Cline, Foster and Fay, Jim. *Parenting With Love and Logic.* Tyndale House Publishing 2006.

3. Fay, Jim and Fay Charles. *Love and Logic Magic for Early Childhood: Practical Parenting From Birth to Six Years.* Tyndale House Publishing, 2000

4. Tabor, James D. "Spanking Children: Does the Bible Tell Me So?" *HUFFPOST.* 26 Nov. 2013, updated 06 Dec 2017, https://www.huffpost.com/entry/spanking-children-does-th_b_5888520

5. Dobson Dr., James. *The New Strong-Willed Child.* Tyndale House Publishing, 2004

6. Dobson. 2004

7. Fay. 2000

8. Tripp, Tedd. *Shepherding a Child's Heart.* Althea Press Publishing, 1995

9. Colossians 3:13-15, Ephesians 4:1-6, Proverbs 19:11, 1 Corinthians 13:4

SECTION 5: WE ARE STRONGER TOGETHER

1. Tripp, 1995

2. Townsend Dr, John. *Who's Pushing Your Buttons.* Thomas Nelson Publishing, 2004

1. Matthew 9:26, John 5:15, Matthew 11:28, Exodus 15:2, Ephesians 3:16

2. "Recognizing God's Power" *Our Daily Bread.* https://ourdailybread.org/resources/recognizing-gods-power/

3. Matthew 11:28-30, 2 Corinthians 12:9-11, 1 Peter 5:7

4. 1 Kings 19

5. Ephesians 6:12, John 1:10, Exodus 14:14

6. Lamott, Anne. *Bird by Bird.* Anchor Books Publishing, 1994

7. Berkeley, Warren E. "There is Nothing New Under the Sun" Ecclesiastes 1:4-11 *The Expository Files* 19.8; August 2012 https://www.bible.ca/ef/expository-ecclesiastes-1-4-11.htm

8. Philippians 4:13, Romans 8:31, Galatians 6:2, 2Corinthians 1:4

ABOUT THE AUTHOR

Tami Overhauser is an author, speaker, and mentor to women. Originally from Southern California, she and her husband Chad live in Austin, Texas and have two grown daughters, Rebekah and Samantha and two teenage sons, Adam and David. When they gather together they can be found laughing in the kitchen, re-  laxing at the lake, and always spoiling their goofy Texas mut, Willie Nelson. Tami teaches about strong faith and strong families and has a passion to see women of all ages fully realize their God-given strength and purpose and help them walk in an abundant life. You can find out more about Tami at Tamioverhauser.com.

Made in the USA
Middletown, DE
06 May 2022

65417462R00149